RESIST

RESIST

essays against a homophobic culture

edited by

Mona Oikawa, Dionne Falconer and Ann Decter

women's PRESS

CANADIAN CATALOGUING IN PUBLICATION DATA
Resist! Essays against a homophobic culture
ISBN 0-88961-197-1
1. Lesbians' writings, Canadian (English).* 2. Lesbians'writings, American.
3. Canadian essays (English) — Women authors.* 4. American essays — Women
authors. 5. Canadian essays (English) — 20th century.* 6. American essays —
20th century. 7. Homophobia -Literary collections. 8. Lesbianism — Literary
collections. I. Oikawa, Mona, 1955- II. Falconer, Dionne III. Decter, Ann, 1956-
PS8235.L47R47 1994 C814'.5408'0353 C94-931683-0
PR9194.5.L47R47 1994

copyright © 1994 the editors: Mona Oikawa, Dionne Falconer and Ann Decter
Individual pieces copyright © 1994 the authors
Publication Credits

*bizarre women, exotic bodies & outrageous sex: or, if annie sprinkle was a
black ho she wouldn't be all that* by karen/miranda augustine was originally
published in *Fireweed: A Feminist Quarterly*, No. 42, Winter 1994 and
Border/Lines: Canada's Magazine of Cultural Studies, No. 32, 1994

Beth Brant's essay, *Physical Prayers* also appears in *Writing as Witness: Essay
and Talk* by Beth Brant, Women's Press, 1994.

Elise Chenier's piece *The Cultivation of Queerness: Parenting My Way into
the 21st Century* first appeared as a Girltalk column in *XTRA* magazine, March
19, 1993.

The poem *Before Me The Land & Water Open* in *Up the Token Pole* by
Chrystos is reprinted from *Fugitive Colors* by Chrystos, Cleveland State
University Press, 1994.

Excerpts from Rachel Epstein's essay, *Lesbian Parenting: Cracking the Shell of
the Nuclear Family* previously appeared in *Healthsharing* magazine.

pièces de résistance by Sheila Gilhooly/barbara findlay was first published in
Sinister Wisdom, winter 1992/93.

The excerpt from Connie Panzarino's book, *The Me in The Mirror* is copyright
Connie Panzarino and reprinted with permission of Seal Press, Seattle,
Washington.

Kathleen Martindale's piece *My (Lesbian) Breast Cancer Story: Can I Get A
Witness?* was previously published in *Fireweed: A Feminist Quarterly of
Writing, Politics, Art and Culture*.

Copy editor: Milagros Santiago
Cover design: Denise Maxwell
Editor photo: Ka Yin Fong

This book was produced by the collective effort of Women's Press.
Women's Press gratefully acknowledges the financial support of the Canada
Council and the Ontario Arts Council.

Printed and bound in Canada
1 2 3 4 5 1998 1997 1996 1995 1994

Contents

Introduction

From its inception this project included two anthologies about lesbians' and bisexual women's resistance to homophobia. The first, *Out Rage*, was a collection of short stories and poetry.

This is its companion, non-fiction, collection. For *Resist!* we wanted essays by women analysing and theorizing their experiences of resisting. We were interested in how women live resistance in their daily lives and how they deal with the contradictions of living in a heterosexist world. It is often presumed that theory is only produced by academics. We know, as lesbians and bisexual women, that analysing and understanding oppression is a tool for our survival.

The writing in this book explores the multiplicity of our identities and the interconnectedness of oppressions. It revels in the power of simple public displays of lesbian affection. It develops theory of sexuality and intimacy while challenging racist sexual representation and colonization. It traces our beginnings in our families of origin to the ones we are creating with lovers, children and friends. It details our working lives, our struggles with institutions, and our strategies for coping and for change. These writers name the pain, the pleasure and the strength of our resistance.

Although, as editors, we may not necessarily agree individually with all the ideas in this collection, we feel it is important that they are published. We hope they will stimulate discussion and generate more writing related to defining ourselves.

Physical Prayers:
Spirituality and Sexuality

Beth Brant

I was told a story.[1] On feast days, after the food was eaten, after the dancing, after the singing prayers, another kind of prayer was begun. Men and women chose who they wished to be partnered with, retired to places on open ground, and commenced the ritual of lovemaking. As the touching, stroking and special play were being enacted, and the sighs and cries were filling the air, the spirit of each individual became a communal prayer of thanksgiving. Sexuality, and the magic ability of our bodies to produce orgasm, was another way to please Creator and ensure all was well and in balance in our world.

As a creative human being who is also Native and lesbian, I will not make distinctions between sexuality and spirituality. To separate would mean to place these two words in competition with each other — to rate them in acquiescence to white-European thought, to deny the power of sex/spirit to my life, my work.

In white North America, sex and spiritual beliefs are commodities that are packaged and sold in the markets of free enterprise. From the golden halls of Vatican City to the strychnine-laced paths of Jonestown, the story is the same — confine the minds and bodies of the followers, especially the minds and bodies of those who are poor and of colour; and of those, make sure the women answer to only one — a white male who can rape at will, who can dole out forgiveness and redemption for a price, who decides which life is expendable and which is not. The emperors of free enterprise claim belief in god and family. Yet, I believe that at the root of their belief system is a hatred of sex. A people who despise sex must also despise their god. Why else do they attempt to make both over in an image that fits a white-male thesis? Why else do they make a vast chasm between god and sex?

As a lesbian, I know that the dominant culture only sees me as a sexually uninhibited creature. As a Native lesbian, I know the dominant culture does not see me at all, or sees an aberration of a "dead" culture. By daring to love and have sex with another like myself, I have stepped beyond any boundary the emperors could have imagined. In the emperors' eyes, sexual freedom means freedom from *them*, a scary thought to be sure. There is no money to be made from the likes of me, except from the porn trade, and even then, lesbian lovemaking is just a prelude to the "real" thing — penetration by a man.

I became a lesbian in my thirty-third year of life. I had had crushes on girls as a youth, and even had a sexual encounter at the age of sixteen with an older woman of eighteen who asked if she could eat my cherry. Of course, I said yes! Curiosity, desire, longing to break any rules, I let my cherry be eaten and look back on that moment with sweet nostalgia. I don't know if I was born a lesbian, and I don't care. I find the recent preoccupation with nature vs. nurture very tiresome and dangerous. In my thirty-third year of life I was a feminist, an activist and largely occupied with discovering all things female. And one of those lovely

discoveries was that I could love women sexually, emotionally and spiritually — and all at once. This is why I choose
to be lesbian. It makes me more complete in myself, and a
whole woman is of much better use to my communities than
a split one.

Now, in my fifty-third year of life I am a feminist, an
activist and a grandmother, and still in the early stages of
discovery and wisdom. But I do think of that distant moment when an older woman of eighteen gave me such
pleasure and allowed me to know my body's desires. I am
not one who wonders "what if?" yet I am fairly certain that
if I had followed my inclination, I might have become that
older woman's "lady," and perhaps would have slipped
easily into the gay life of the fifties. I was/am very much a
child of my class. I would have gotten a job as a cashier or
as a saleslady. My lover would have worked on the line, and
we would have made a home in a fairly traditional
butch/femme way, I probably never would have become a
writer, much less a woman who says the word "lesbian" out
loud in front of strangers! And my being Native, my being
Mohawk, might have been a source of distant amusement
or puzzlement to my lover. We would have been women of
our time and class. I expect my family would have reacted
in much the same way they did years later — accepting a
white woman into the family because I loved her. But our
lives would have been hidden from the dominant culture.

The blending of Native and lesbian, which to me has
been a sensual and pleasing journey, is not so pleasant to
some of my own Native sisters and brothers of the heterosexual persuasion. I could discount their anger, and/or
off-handedly blame colonialism — which *is* to blame — but
I desire to look further into the heart of this anger and
imagine a revelation that could possibly transform us as

individuals and community members. This is something I cannot do alone.

I don't know if all First Nations have words or expressions to connote their Two-Spirit members. I cannot find a word in Mohawk that describes me; however, Mohawk is a woman language in that if gender is not described in other terms, it is assumed to be female. Perhaps a Two-Spirit was not an *uncommon*-enough occurrence to be granted a special word. And perhaps a gay man was known by a female term, and a lesbian like myself was a woman among many other women. I *am* certain, though, that I am not the first Mohawk lesbian to walk this earth, and that certainty has helped ease the pain I feel when confronted by another Native who discounts me on account of my sexuality. I also don't know if all First Nations gave special or exalted status to its Two-Spirit citizens. There are some stories of Two-Spirits being revered *because* of their blurred gender and uncompromising way of living within their clan or tribal unit.[2] These stories are important ones to treasure and repeat to our young, but I think they cannot take the place of living and breathing lesbians and gay men who can be role models if we are able to jump over the chasm that homophobia has blasted into our Nations. And many of us find ourselves at the edge of this precipice that separates us from our beloved people.

Those first whitemen who stumbled across our world had limited vision of what they were seeing — peoples who lived with the sun and the moon. Peoples whose time was not measured by hourglasses or clocks, but by what was happening on the earth and in the sky. Peoples who looked at animals to judge when a season was passing and changing. Peoples who acted together, in consensus, because to do otherwise was unthinkable and foolish. Peoples who were not ashamed or afraid of bodily functions or sexual acts. Peoples who had a rhythm that pulsed to that of the Earth. The whiteman saw none of these, except for the unashamed celebration of sexuality. They were so spellbound by this they filled reams of paper on this subject. The Jesuits especially gloried in recounting every sexual act. The Spanish and French wrote home to Europe about the sexual "looseness" of Native women. Of course, these men did not mention the word "rape." Nor did they write back home about our spirituality, except to call us "heathens." Neither explorer nor religious saw our physical presence in *our* own context, nor did they hear the prayers that were a joyous song to being part of the natural. To this day, the whiteman continues to look at Indigenous Peoples from *their* context, fitting us into *their* limited and limiting view of Earth.

The church and the state have long worked as consorts in the colonization of Aboriginal peoples. With the guns came the Bible. With the Bible came the whisky. With the whisky came addiction and government over our affairs. With the government came the reserves, and loathing of all that was natural. With loathing came the unnatural; the internalization of all they told us about ourselves. And the beliefs hold fast in some. There are christian Indians, and there are homophobic Indians.

In speaking with an Elder from Tyendinaga, I asked her how things had changed in her ninety-six years of life. She started to cry and said, "We learned all sorts of bad things from the whites. Now we no longer love each other." And perhaps this is the key to understanding homophobia within my Nation. The love that was natural in our world has become unnatural, as we become more consumed by the white world and the values therein. Our sexuality has been colonized, sterilized, whitewashed. Our sense of spirit has been sterilized, colonized, made over to pander to a growing consumer need for quick and easy redemption. What the dominant culture has never been able to comprehend is that spirit/sex/prayer/flesh/religion/natural is who I am as a Two-Spirit. *Now we no longer love each other.* What a triumph for the whiteman and the cultural enslavement he brought to the First Nations. When we fight amongst ourselves as to who is a better Indian, who is a more traditional Indian, we are linking arms with the ones who would just as soon see us dead. Homophobia has *no* justification within our Nations.

My partner and I have a small cottage on Walpole Island in Ontario. Walpole Island is held by a confederacy known as the Council of Three Fires — Potawatomi, Ottawa, Ojibwa — and since it comprises several islands, there are numerous canals and tiny channels of water where only a canoe can get through. Denise and I canoe every chance we get. We both love the steady movement of paddles in the water, the sounds of marsh birds, the glimpse of turtles under the water, the sun on our faces, that wondrous smell of fertility all around us, and sometimes the special gift of finding a feather or a nest floating by us.

On this day, we found a small patch of dry land with a black willow growing straight out of the earth. There was a noisy Red-wing flying in and out of the branches. We hesitated before beaching the canoe, knowing how protective these birds are, and not wanting to disturb him or the nest he might be guarding. But he flew away and we climbed out onto the land. We talked, ate our lunch, breathed the air, then lay under the willow and touched each other, kissed, made love between us. As I felt the first tremors of orgasm take hold of me, a Blue Heron entered my body and I became her. Each pulse of orgasm was a flap of wings, a preparation for flight, and as orgasm took hold of me, I felt myself lifting from the ground, wings gathering strength, flying. I opened my long, yellow beak and gave a cry. Later, I asked Denise if she had heard the voice of Heron. "No, dearest, I only heard yours."

In this moment of time and place, Heron had chosen me to communicate her cries of freedom, power and joy in being the magnificent creature she is. She told me that her joy was mine, and mine was hers. This is physical prayer. This is creation. This is what cannot be stolen from me, or frightened out of me. Although Heron has not come to me again in that especial intimate way, when I see her flying, or standing still in water, the long curve of her neck sparkling and shimmering in the sunlight, I feel, once again, the wonder of the great mysteries that are part of the natural order of my world.

Those people who despise sex also despise Heron and others like her. The need to "have dominion over the earth" is not a natural or a healthy way to be on this earth. There have been numerous books and articles written by white feminists to describe the hatred of women that is carried over to nature. If men can't kill all women, they will attempt to kill all that lives, especially that which comes from Mother Earth. While I agree with some of this theorizing, I feel it does not encompass Aboriginal thought, or any theories about lesbianism. There is also no mention of enchantment, or to use a better word, *orenda*, a Mohawk description of what cannot be explained but is accepted as the natural order of life. Perhaps even in feminism it is too difficult to give up a belief in the eurocentric way of living and being. A Native man may be sexist, but still he lovingly tends corn and beans, says a prayer of forgiveness for killing a deer or moose for his family, and believes fully in the power of magic in his life.

I am reminded of a gathering of Native writers that took place in 1992. A Mohawk man gave a speech in which he exhibited the worst kinds of white-leftist harangue. Some of the women in the audience were angry at his patronizing behaviour and obvious sexism. It was discussed who would speak to him. *I* was selected — because I am Mohawk, because I am his elder by ten or fifteen years. I did speak to him. He listened, albeit angrily at first. And I knew that this was a man who cared passionately about the environment, about children, who spoke the language of our ancestors, but nevertheless had internalized the European/Marxist thought of male domination, and the macho posturing that comes with it. Sexism is a learned behaviour, not a natural behaviour in Aboriginal cultures. And one can call himself traditional and still be sexist.

The Longhouse religion of recent use comes from the Code of Handsome Lake, or *Gai'wiio'*. Handsome Lake, Seneca Nation, was a reformed alcoholic who had many visions of a new religion. He was born in 1735. In his later years he was terribly aggrieved at the havoc brought to his people by the whiteman. Being a man who cared deeply and strongly about his people, Handsome Lake introduced many Christian-based concepts and "ways" that he exhorted the People to follow. Among those messages were "marriage" between men and women, the Christian concept of adultery and "forgiveness" of it (if committed by a husband), the disbanding of animal societies and the dances to honour these Totems, the ban against homosexuality, the confessing of witchcraft and the cease of such practice, and the ban on women to employ herbs and medicines for the purpose of abortion or birth control. It is interesting to me that witchcraft, as seen by Handsome Lake, was a female activity that involved the seduction of men to perform ugly acts, but the practice of curing and healing was a male activity; thus, these practitioners were known as Medicine Men. I find this curiously christian and antithetical to old Iroquois belief, where women held the knowledge of healing and the mysteries of earth and cosmos. Before his death in 1815, Handsome Lake carried his message to the People of the Iroquois Confederacy and it has held firm among many of the People. I find nothing traditionally Onkwehonwe in this religion. Homophobia can thrive in the uneasy mixture of christian thought and Aboriginal belief. And it does. If sexism is a learned behaviour, so is homophobia. They can be unlearned, if the desire is present. Some of the unlearning has to begin with us, the Two-Spirits.

Much of the self-hatred we carry within us is centuries old. This self-hatred is so coiled within itself, we often cannot distinguish the racism from the homophobia from the sexism. We carry the stories of our grandmothers, our ancestors. And some of these stories are ugly and terrorizing. And some are beautiful testaments to endurance and dignity. We must learn to emulate this kind of testimony. Speaking ourselves out loud — for our people, for ourselves. To deny our sexuality is to deny our part in creation.

The denial of sexuality and those who live according to their sexuality is almost unspeakable. It has been named "homophobia," but that bland word does not tell of the blasphemous acts committed against us in the name of religion and state. I use the word "blasphemy" because that is what it is — a defilement of all that is spirit-filled and ceremonial. I also believe that the hatred and violence that is directed against us is a result of the hatred against their god. It must be difficult to follow a doctrine that orders them to live perfect, sex-empty, anti-sensual lives, then turn around and behold *us,* the perverts that god also made. This must drive the homophobes insane with anger. We get away with it and are not punished by this god that exhorts *them* to be good, or else! Of course, the more fundamentalist types say AIDS is a punishment. But even this theology is falling by the wayside as more and more heterosexuals and children are being infected. If one hates the god who made them, they can turn that hatred inward and outward to people who are not like them. I have often thought that racism, sexism, homophobia are results of a giant cultural and religious inferiority psychosis. I realize this is not an original theory, but I adhere to its basic premise.

Those of us who are Two-Spirit do not believe we are better, smarter, more spiritual or more *Indian* than others. We do not proselytize, promise salvation and redemption, sell amulets or holy cards to a heaven. We do not promise a better life by saving heterosexual souls. We do not tell stories of men dying on crosses to incite guilt. We do live our lives in the best way we can. We do attempt to appreciate the unique position we have in our communities. We are not "just like everybody else." That line is for those who are still trying to prove themselves worthy of the dominant culture's approval. I think the 1992 March on Washington that took place in the United States made many mistakes in trying to look, and act "just like everybody else." One of the more endearing and daring facets of being gay/lesbian/bi is the outlandishness that permeates our communities. What's wrong in being an outlaw? I will not prove myself to anyone. I am a mother — a lesbian mother. I am a grandmother — a lesbian grandmother. I am the lesbian daughter of my mother and father. I am the lesbian lover of women. I am the lesbian partner of Denise. I am the lesbian being who welcomes Heron, Turtle and Moose into her life. I am the lesbian being who prays with words, my heart and my body. I am a Two-Spirit woman of the Mohawk Nation. I am a lesbian who listens to the spirits who guide me. I am a Two-Spirit who walks this path my ancestors cleared for us. If I can clear more brush and cut through thickets, I will. For I feel that we also make tradition in our various and varied communities and Nations. This tradition is generous and welcoming. It is a tradition of wholeness and honour. It is a tradition of remembrance and fidelity.

Endnotes

1. In a conversation with Donna Marchand, Native lesbian writer and student of law, she brought up the concept of orgasm as a natural resource. I thank her most gratefully for sharing the brilliance of her mind.
2. Will Roscoe, *The Zuni Man-Woman* (University of New Mexico Press).

Mother Tongue

Ann Yuri
Ueda

This piece is dedicated to my mother, who took me to the library for the first time when I was four years old and began my life-long love of words. Even though today we do not speak to each other, I will always remember you and your dream of wanting to write.

For many years, the only translation I had for my Japanese middle name was the one given to me by my mother when I thought to ask.

I remember watching a Japanese-language soap opera on TV with the English subtitles endlessly inching along the bottom of the screen. After dinner on Sunday nights, my parents chose to watch all of the four-hour block of TV programs originally produced and broadcast in Japan. We only had one TV then, so I could either watch or go do something else. Occasionally bored enough to be curious, I would watch with my parents to understand why they faithfully tuned in to these programs on the one night a week they were shown, on this one station in the greater Los Angeles viewing area.

I couldn't "get it," finding it too much work for my eyes to jump from the subtitles to the action occurring above. Behind me, my parents sat on the couch watching the screen, reading the translation and hearing some of the dialogue.

Now, I understand why they watched these programs. I remember them conferring back and forth, translating words, phrases; checking the romanized Japanese-English dictionary for words they didn't know; searching the map atlas of Japan for the location of cities and other places mentioned. The Sunday TV programs were the way my parents tried to stem the loss of a language they barely knew and hadn't spoken except long ago in a hybrid mix with English, when their respective parents were still alive. I suspect it was also a way of sharing something my parents had in common — belonging to the second generation of Japanese living in America.

During this time, I began to understand that other languages and words could be translated into English for my comprehension because I was monolingual. One Sunday night, perhaps because he was bored, my father showed me how to write our last name in Japanese and explained its meaning in English:

上　　ue — upper

田　　da — ricefield, paddy

I remember not being impressed by this translation, envisioning a paddy on a hillside somewhere, filled with water. No matter how creative I tried to be, the picture just wasn't interesting. Besides, no one ever asked me what our family name meant so I filed my father's translation away.

I had to ask what my middle name meant in English, and it was my mother who gave me the translation, explaining Yuri meant lily flower. I remember not being impressed by this translation, either, but would be able to use this information, because I was often asked what my middle name meant. No one ever asked me to write Yuri in Japanese, so I didn't think to ask; I don't think my parents knew the corresponding kanji, since neither one volunteered to show me how.

I've always been uncomfortable with having a middle name that translated into lily flower. The translation just didn't fit who I was. I was a tomboy growing up: I hated dolls, always wore pants, played rough with the neighbourhood kids, never had music or dance or art lessons like other girls, hung out with my father, and played in the dirt. It was hard for me to imagine myself as a lily flower. Sometimes I got teased by kids who thought my middle name **was** Lily, but I learned to give the translation with a particular look or tone that quickly communicated the subject of my middle name was officially closed to further discussion.

For a long time, the only saving grace of my middle name was the lack of the -ko suffix common on the end of Japanese women's names. This suffix denotes the diminutive form of the name, roughly translating into "little girl" or "child." As a lesbian with a certain reputation to protect and a tomboy past, I was certainly glad not to have that baggage hanging onto my middle name. As difficult as it was for me to imagine myself as a lily flower, there was no way I could accept my middle name ending in -ko. I didn't want to be a "little" anything.

I want to make it clear that I was never ashamed or embarrassed about having a Japanese middle name, although for most of my life I have not been proud or comfortable about being Japanese American. Instead, my middle name has always been a wonderful reminder of my ethnic heritage and family life. This apparent paradox can be explained because of my mother.

When I was younger and still living at home, I could always tell my mother's disposition when she called out my name to summon me. If she was mad, I would hear, "Ann! Come here," in her stern tone. But when she was in a loving mood or needing to call me for any other reason, I'd hear "Ann Yuri," or simply "Yuri." Until I moved out of the house, I learned to wince and wished to run away when I heard "Ann," but knew things were OK if I also heard "Yuri." Yuri became part of a special language shared by my mother and me, a language made up of some words, but mostly of moments filled with the tone of our voices and gestures and looks shared between a nisei mother and her sansei daughter.

Of course, no one else but my mother called me Yuri, but no one else could ever say it like she did, the way it's supposed to be said, the way I remember it, the way I like Yuri to be said.

Since coming out to my parents almost five years ago, we've not spoken at all. They haven't taken well the news that their only child is a lesbian and an activist. I respect their wish to not be in contact with me, but I do miss them. I especially miss hearing my mother call out "Ann Yuri," and I wonder if I'll ever hear her say my name again in her particular tone and voice before one of us dies. There is still no one else who calls me Yuri.

I remember a story about my middle name my mother must have told me when I was younger. It's been so long since I heard the story that I remember the words more vividly than I do the person who actually spoke the words. The story has to do with the missing -ko. I think it was my mother who wanted to name me Yuri and my paternal grandmother who wanted to name me the more traditional Yuriko. (It is not known how my father felt about my naming or whose side he supported; his ambivalence or absence seems pretty typical in the naming of a daughter.) If this story is true, then my middle name shows my mother won: my middle name means lily flower in Japanese and represents a small victory of my mother's will claimed between those two generations. Sometimes, I think I can feel the strength of her will in my name, in my life, in my activism, especially now that I remain separated from her by her strict silence. In these moments, I wonder why my mother cannot look at me and see that I am still her daughter.

I'm not sure why my mother wanted to leave off the -ko. I can't talk to her to find out the answers and verify the truth. But happily, I am a writer and have drafted up many of my own conclusions to ease some of the pain I've felt during the years I haven't spoken with my parents.

I like to think my mother wanted my middle name to remind me of my Japanese heritage, and that I would always be a woman in my own full right, no one's little girl or made diminutive in any way. And when it is my turn to name my children, I will also omit the -ko ending for my own daughters.

That is my own myth-making, the personal meaning I've attributed to this partially true/myth story. Whatever the truth may be or whenever I find it out, I'm certainly grateful my mother named me Yuri.

I'm twenty-nine years old as I write this, and I've never met anyone else who had Yuri as her first or middle name. Admittedly, the potential pool of Japanese women I knew was small, but I kept searching anyway.

I think I was looking for my namesake to comfort an almost perpetual sense I have always had of being alone, of being different from everyone else. As far back as I can remember, I've always wanted to be a writer. I've always been an outspoken activist for various grassroots causes. I was in the fourth grade when I realized I liked my girlfriends more than the boys in class, a preference that never changed and resulted in my coming out as a lesbian at age twenty-three.

In short, I have always been a non-traditional woman, a status reinforced by my decision to accept my sexuality and come out as a lesbian. Having a non-traditional Japanese middle name, then, has been appropriate, but perhaps not in the ways my mother intended or even anticipated.

But looking Japanese has made the choices about who I would be and the life I would live more difficult and lonely for me, because of the dearth of other Japanese women to serve as role models for me. I never knew how it would look to be a Japanese American writer, a Japanese American activist, a Japanese American lesbian, a non-traditional Japanese American woman. Each decision I've made, each identity I've claimed, has occurred without these guides, simply because it had to, for me to remain happy, sane, whole, healthy.

Yet, I still felt alone. I still needed to know there were other Japanese and Japanese American women like me. I needed my predecessors, my role models, my own kindred sister spirits tied more tightly together because of our shared ethnic heritage.

Lately, I have become more comfortable with my Japanese ancestry. And as a woman writer, I've been inspired to read the writings of other Japanese women. Because I did not ever know my maternal and paternal grandparents before they died, I have tried to understand something about them by studying the Japan they lived in before immigrating to America around the turn of this century. I've combined both interests by reading *To Live and To Write, Selections by Japanese Women Writers, 1913-1938,* edited by Yukiko Tanaka.

In many ways, these women writers were very non-traditional, and it is unlikely my own grandmothers were like them in life or spirit, instead confined to the traditional roles of daughter-wife-mother, roles filled with constant sacrificing for others, silent suffering and dream deferring.

However, I am encouraged by reading about these women writers, to know that they were ardent, thoughtful, articulate and political feminists in their lives, loves and writing. So, while perhaps not like my grandmothers, I recognize their spirits and writing as akin to my own. In fact, because my works are autobiographical and draw deeply on my personal experiences as a sansei lesbian activist writer, I find my own work continues a tradition that is well established and recognized in Japanese literature. I write with a spirit shared by other women and men who also shaped what they wrote by the lives they led. As a woman writer of Japanese descent, then, I am part of another mainstream that is not white and is not American.

And behold! One of the women in Tanaka's anthology is named Yuriko Miyamoto!

In Miyamoto's biography compiled by Tanaka, I read my namesake was a leader of the intellectuals at the end of World War II and had a long literary career considered rare for Japanese women writers. Tanaka likens Miyamoto's writing to that of Simone de Beauvoir so similar are their life experiences and subject matter.

Reading between Tanaka's lines, I surmise Yuriko was involved in a relationship with Yoshiko Yuasa, a journalist and scholar of Russian literature. Tanaka explains that

Yoshiko, a lesbian, influenced Yuriko profoundly, and that the two "shared each other's lives for seven years," in which "during the first few [years], they lived together in a large rented house." Yoshiko "became a source of inspiration and encouragement" for Yuriko, helping her to finish *Nobuko*, her first novel, and begin the divorce from her first husband. Yuriko joined Yoshiko on a trip to the Soviet Union in 1928, returning to Japan three years later as an avowed Marxist and incorporating her communist beliefs into her writing. Yuriko would later be jailed and tortured by the Japanese government for these same beliefs. Tanaka does not say what happened to Yoshiko, and Yuriko would several years later enter into her second marriage. Yuriko would write about her relationship with Yoshiko in *Signpost*, Yuriko's autobiography.

Nobuko, *Signpost* and *Two Gardens* (the latter being Yuriko's next major novel after *Nobuko*) would complete her "autobiographical trilogy," the three volumes bearing "witness to a woman's struggle for personal freedom and growth and her developing political consciousness." According to Tanaka, "the novels of this trilogy are also particularly important for illuminating Yuriko's concerns as a woman and as an artist."

Yuriko died at age 52, and:

> At the time of her death she was widely regarded as the conscience of the intellectuals and a writer deeply concerned with the condition of Japanese women. A writer devoted to her personal relationships and political commitments as well as to her art, she is remembered today both for her written works and her lifetime of political activism.[1]

Suddenly, I have a role model in the life and writings of Yuriko Miyamoto. I want to learn more about her and read her writing in the original Japanese, a task that will entail learning the Japanese language, including the 2,000 kanji which are essential for reading comprehension. In many ways, I understand Yuriko's life because it so closely parallels my own. I'd like to think my own mother named me after a woman like Yuriko Miyamoto to embolden me to live my life as fully as my namesake.

I recently came across another Yuri, another sansei woman writer: Lydia Yuri Minatoya, author of *Talking To High Monks in the Snow*. Although not a lesbian, Lydia and I share certain commonalities as American sanseis, including the persistent sense of being different, a sense made more discomforting by growing up and living in mostly all-white communities.

The book, subtitled "An Asian American Odyssey," recounts Lydia's childhood, filled with mounting self-hatred directed at her Japanese identity and intimate moments shared with her parents and extended family members, uncovering hidden family secrets. Her book also describes trips made to Japan, China and Nepal as an adult woman, and the people she meets on her travels.

Lydia writes with a style I identify as the new voice of Asian-American literature, a distinctive and rich voice enhanced by her Japanese American identity. In touch with her emotions and with a fine command of descriptive details, Lydia offers us her first book filled with insight, humour, gracefulness, wisdom, and tears of sadness and celebration. Such richness makes her book impossible to easily breeze through in several sittings, and I found myself crying often after reading passages that spoke of my own experiences and feelings. Her book is really that good.

I bought Lydia's book to support another sansei woman writer, and to read if she'd written the book I want to write about, my own experiences in Japan as a sansei lesbian (she hadn't, naturally).

But most of all, I bought the book because on the inside page I saw her full name. I had never before seen my middle name on an American Library of Congress catalogue card commonly found in books, and I found the sight of Lydia Yuriko Minatoya quite exciting! Upon seeing Lydia's middle name, I wanted to know if she would explain the translation her own mother gave for Yuriko. Almost toward the end, Lydia offers her mother's interpretation:

> "What does my name look like?" I question my mother. I am ten years old. It is an August afternoon. My glass of lemonade sweats in my hand.
>
> My mother focuses on her task. She is seated at the kitchen table, translating correspondence for my father's pharmaceutical firm. With a stiff brush she is painting strange characters onto translucent, wrinkled airmail paper. The ink smells sharp and acrid.
>
> I wait. I know my mother cannot resist an opportunity to bestow her cultural knowledge.
>
> My mother reaches for a fresh piece of paper. It whispers in complaint. "Come Yuri-chan," she says. "I will teach you to write your name."
>
> She dips the brush in ink. Her forearm hovers above the paper circling before it descends. "Yu-ri," she says making the strokes, "cle-ver." She looks at the character with satisfaction. "I chose this character for its special meaning."
>
> "Clever? It means clever?" I am disappointed.
>
> "Other mother write Yuri this way." She flicks her

wrist and another character appears. "To them, the meaning is lily flower."

"That's pretty!"

"Take that glass to the sink. It drips. Besides, too much sweet is not good for young girls." My mother is annoyed. She deliberately has named me "clever" and I am too stupid to see why.

"Why didn't you name me lily flower?" I persist.

"Too many flowers already. In America, it is better to prepare a child to be clever — to be open to the world, to accept imagination, to see the unseen. A flower girl gets picked. A flower girl gets trampled. A clever girl gets prize."

I make what my mother calls my unpleasant American face. I am sceptical. I know nice Japanese names that mean something important, like Michiko — beautiful and intelligent. Clever, hmmph. Clever is what you want in your dog.[2]

Yuri also means...clever? I rush to my dictionary where I read:

clever *adj*. 1. Mentally quick and resourceful. 2. Quick-witted. 3. Dexterous. [Poss. ME *cliver*, expert in seizing.] Synonyms: clever, bright, alert, intelligent, sharp, smart.[3]

Yu-ri. Cle-ver. I don't read very many written pieces translated into English, because often the English version doesn't feel right to me and therefore I don't like the work. I wonder if the translation really says the same thing the author intended in the original language; there are always nuances that do not translate. But this other meaning of my middle name fits, feels right. While Lydia wanted to be a lily flower because it sounded pretty, I wanted a middle name with a greater spirit to capture my own then-burgeoning sense of self. I always knew there was another translation to my middle name, one that I would instantly be comfortable with, the translation offering me an expanded sense of pride, purpose and strength.

Clever does that. It is still the same name — Yuri — only I've reinterpreted the given so instead of writing:

百合   Yuri — lily flower

I can also write:

由利   Yuri — clever, reason

I recently began studying kanji, tackling the seventy-six characters which comprise the set taught to first graders in Japanese elementary schools.[4] I am learning to make and recognize characters for: rain, life spirit, sound, tree, the numbers one through ten. As I study, I find that there are actually several other kanji I can also use to represent my middle name. After research and consideration, I have decided to change the kanji to:

 Joy, pleasure. Composed of the radicals (root characters which give a sense of the actual meaning of the kanji):

忄   heart, feelings.

俞   Phonetic character (gives the pronunciation of the kanji) "convey," giving the "YU" sound.

王里　Reason, principle, rational; meaning
心　of concentration also indicated.
Composed of the radicals:

王　jewel.

里　phonetic character "village"
or "native place," giving the "RI" sound.

This is, I feel, the final iteration of my middle name. The meaning of joy, emotion may seem to contradict that of reason, intellect, but as a Japanese American Virgo with Cancer rising, the mixture represents quite accurately my internal reality, how I perceive and deal with the world around me. Choosing these kanji will help to remind me that neither feeling nor intellect should ever predominate, that instead the two should work together in harmony.

I especially treasure the phonetic component of "RI," meaning "village" or "native place," for so often I feel that I have no home. I cannot return to my family's ancestral home in Japan for I am too American and appreciate the kind of choices available to me here. America, my birth-place, is not my home, either. As a lesbian of colour, the typically all-white gay/lesbian/bisexual/transgender community is not home. And, for now, I cannot return to my childhood home until my parents decide otherwise. Over the years, then, home has come to truly exist within my heart, and now it resonates in the way I write my middle name and how I envision it when I hear or think of Yuri.

It has been over a year since this renaming/rewriting of my middle name, and some incredible things have happened. I have decided to go to Japan for the first time in 1996, on an extended stay when I will write my first book detailing my experiences there. I have begun learning both the spoken and written forms of Japanese, a task I put off for so many years because of the ingrained shame and internalized racism I had learned because I am Japanese. I have begun to meet other non-traditional Japanese women living in Japan and overseas, whose own stories provide me with encouragement and points of personal reflection. I want to research further into the lives of Yuriko Miyamoto and other Japanese women writers who lived and wrote prior to World War II. I am incorporating Japanese themes and literary techniques into my own writing.

And, suddenly, my mother is not the only significant Japanese woman I know in my life, and this knowing helps me to somehow move beyond the silence and estrangement characterizing my current relationship with my parents. My mother and family are no longer the immediate ties to my Japanese identity; I no longer need to depend solely on them to tell me who I am or where I originally came from.

Finding out this other meaning and other way to write Yuri has started in me a process of understanding who I am as a Japanese woman, outside of the context provided by my parents and extended family, almost all of whom reject me in some way because I am a lesbian or else support my parents' silence towards me. The translation of my middle name has finally made me bold enough to confront my Japanese identity among other Japanese and Japanese society. As a result, I am finding, understanding and appreciating the nuances of my being, feeling and thinking which, even after three generations and 100 years of the American experience, are still innately and intuitively Japanese. And all these uncoverings and translations also ''fit,'' feel right. Perhaps in my search, Mother Tongue has become Women's Tongue, this woman's tongue. And with my tongue, with my words, with these two languages struggling to find life and meaning within me, I am crafting my writing…I will not be silent any more, and I cannot die until I finish telling all the stories contained within me.

"To be open to the world, to accept imagination, to see the unseen. A clever girl gets prize," Lydia's mother explains.

For me, those words have been my guiding principles for a life lived as a lesbian, as a sansei woman writer, as a Japanese American activist, as a non-traditional Japanese woman. Not having readily identifiable role models appropriate for me has mandated that I be the visionary who dares to dream of those things not yet real, who sees those things which remain unseen by others, who works to make her dreams and visions real for herself, her family and her community. Those words have allowed me to be fully all I see and dream. For me, the prize has been my life.

Perhaps when choosing my middle name, my mother could sense my own clever spirit and decided to name me Yuri. Or perhaps I sensed another meaning for my middle name and strove to be the incarnation of this translation.

When I was old enough to finally ask, perhaps my mother told me only the more common interpretation of lily flower, knowing all along the other meaning, too. Perhaps by then she realized she could keep it her secret, knowing I would eventually come across this hidden interpretation.

The joy of learning for me has always been self-discovery and self-revelation, which only makes my new-found information even more valuable and memorable. Perhaps my mother knew this, too, recognizing this joy in herself and seeing it as one of the many ties between this mother and her daughter.

Uncovering this other meaning — Yuri as lily flower and

clever — and discovering kanji for my middle name which describes who I feel I am: both have been unexpected finds on my life's journey, beautiful jewels sparkling in my soul, part of the light within me which now burns brighter and longer for this knowing.

Endnotes

1. Yuriko Tanaka, ed. *To Live and To Write, Selections by Japanese Women Writers, 1913-1938* (Seattle: Seal Press, 1987), 45. All quotes about Yuriko Miyamoto come from this anthology.
2. Lydia Yuriko Minatoya, *Talking to High Monks in the Snow, An Asian American Odyssey* (New York: Harper Collins Publishers, Inc., 1992), 225-226. All quotes in the section on Lydia Yuriko Minatoya come from this book.
3. *The American Heritage Dictionary*, 2d ed. (Boston: Houghton Mifflin Company, 1983). The definition of "clever" is taken from this dictionary.
4. I want to thank Misako Watanabe for explaining to me that the actual kanji used to represent spoken Japanese can vary, since many of the kanji have different readings. (For example, "YU" in Yuri can be written using any one of eight possible kanji, as can "RI.") If she had not said this, it would have taken me much longer to find the kanji for my middle name and also to begin studying kanji on my own.

Translation for words used:

Nisei — Second generation Japanese American.

Sansei — Third generation Japanese American.

Kanji — Formal writing system in the Japanese language based on the Chinese characters which were imported to Japan.

–chan — A suffix added to Japanese girls' and women's names denoting affection and tenderness; used between parents and their children, and between close friends.

Thoughts on Heterosexism, Queerness and Outlaws

Mary Louise Adams

"Heterosexism" is not an everyday term. It's not printed in the newspaper, it doesn't appear in my dictionary and it has yet to make it onto the agenda of my chosen political party or the curriculum at the local school. Outside progressive circles, heterosexism is pretty much an unknown concept, although I did hear Peter Gzowski stumble over it recently on CBC national radio.

Inside progressive circles, heterosexism, as both a concept and a term, has a better foothold. Still, it doesn't slip off the tongue as easily as terms like "sexism" or "racism" or "class oppression," as easily as the more frequently used term "homophobia." Too often the distinction between "heterosexism" and "homophobia" gets lost in progressive "right-on-speak." The two words tend to be used interchangeably to refer to all the bad stuff that happens to lesbians and gay men. This lack of specificity is more than just a sign of sloppy language, it also signals limitations in our understanding of what it means to be lesbians and gay men in this society.

Homophobia refers to people's fears of homosexuality; homophobia is a condition of individuals. It's a concept that leads some lesbians and gay men, and many of our non-homo supporters, to conclusions like: if only homophobes understood us better, they'd treat us better. In contrast, the notion of heterosexism encourages us to look past individuals to the larger social-political system in which we are all implicated. Heterosexism refers to the institutionalization and privileging of particular forms of heterosexuality. What this means is that those of us who don't define ourselves as straight don't just suffer at the hands of selected, unenlightened individuals; we live and work within a system that requires the subordination of our desires so it can function efficiently. An analysis of heterosexism suggests that we need fundamental change in the way our society is structured before lesbians, gay men, bisexuals and other sexual non-conformers lose their status as oddities and cease to suffer the consequences of that marginalized position.

Heterosexism refers to a pernicious cultural process, what Gayle Rubin called "obligatory heterosexuality" in a 1977 article,[1] what Adrienne Rich later called "compulsory heterosexuality."[2] Heterosexism points to social, political and economic factors, and to the ways they marginalize a *variety* of groups, including lesbians and gay men, who don't meet the cultural dictates of normative heterosexuality, whatever they happen to be at any given moment.

Heterosexism flags a hierarchical relationship that is under constant negotiation. As a relational term, heterosexism calls into question the dichotomizing of sexuality into two opposite categories. At the same time it gives us room to recognize the large fuzzy area in the middle of the gay/straight divide, to recognize the overlaps, the contradictions. In contrast, homophobia directs the weight of inquiry to one side of a simple equation. To my mind, homophobia is a clear product of heterosexist discourses that assume a clean split between so-called opposite sexualities. Fortunately, life is more complicated than that.

Sexuality operates in remarkably fluid ways in both individual lives and social discourse. The boundaries between sexualities are neither easily maintained nor policed Definitions of appropriate or normative sexuality — of the heterosexual ideal — while ever changing and inherently unstable, are very narrow and widely exclusionary. Heterosexism, then, isn't the exclusive territory of lesbians and gay men. It is too simple to say that the opposition highlighted by the concept of heterosexism is the gay/straight one. Rather it is an 'idealized' heterosexuality versus everything else, which might include lesbian and gay sex, interracial sex, prostitution, bisexuality, het promiscuity, intergenerational sex, transsexuality, transvestism, etc. It's a divide that might tentatively be classified as queer versus unqueer.

Queer stuff

We've heard a lot about queers over the last few years, and about queerness. Queer nations, queer theorists, queer movements, queer conferences. Like any politically charged term, it means vastly different things to different people. For many, it flags the in-your-face brashness of a get-used-to-it activism. For some, it's a way of throwing into question the rigidities of current lesbian and gay "institutions." For some, it's the conscious expression of a sharply defined identity politics. For others, and I count myself in here, it's an antidote to the limitations of identity politics.

At the very least, "queer" challenges us to think about its opposition: what is it that we mean by "unqueer"?

Certainly, it isn't captured by the simple category "straight" or heterosexual. Queerness is counterposed by something far more specific: the kind of sexuality that's expressed in monogamous, heterosexual, single-race marriages that produce children and are sanctioned by the state, the church and much of the media.

I assume that many "queers" would disagree with me here, not wanting our category to be quite so inclusive; there are, indeed, very few people who fit the culturally-endorsed unqueer ideal. But, the point I'm trying to make isn't about the correct usage of a contested term. Instead, I'm fishing for a way to think culturally and politically about sexual identities and sexual behaviours. Is it useful to think about similarities, without glossing over differences, between the various groups of people — perhaps a majority of us — who fall outside the boundaries of sexual acceptability? In understanding these marginal groups as a collectivity, can we achieve a better understanding of the norm and how mainstream discourses play themselves out by regulating our lives?

Theoretically, this way of mobilizing a broadly defined "queerness" appeals to me very much. I'm much less clear about what it might mean in actual practice. Perhaps we'd see the formation of some kind of broad-based coalition of non-conformers and perverts, a constant challenging of what's taken for normal, of the boundaries of the so-called respectable desires. I also see queerness as a way of countering simplistic identity-based political strategies that have resulted in, for instance, the addition of the word "bisexual" to the names of already existing lesbian and gay organizations. What are the implications of this kind of add-'em-on organizing as a representational tactic for a newly profiled bisexual identity, or for tenuously held lesbian and gay turf, symbolic and cultural? On a gut level, I find this approach to sexual politics decidedly unqueer.

Instead of piggy-backing bisexual organizing onto gay and lesbian work, I'd suggest parallel enterprises and more complex explorations of the categories, indeed of our need to categorize sexuality. Where do the categories overlap? How do they contradict each other? How are they distinct? How does the definition of one create a boundary for the others? Using the notion of queerness to look at similarities is not a process of collapsing a variety of sexual identities on top of each other. The similarities we need to look for are in our experiences of sexual marginalization under a heterosexual hegemony, as Gary Kinsman has called it.[3] Beyond that we need to detail the myriad ways people live outside socially approved definitions of heterosexuality. The point is not to show that we are all the same, but to show, in fact, how different we are and what a huge group we are. The obfuscation of this point is one of the ways that heterosexism successfully makes its claim to dominance, in the same way that white people, who are a global minority, talk about ourselves as if we were a statistical majority.

Part of the problem in even imagining the possibilities of a broadly defined queerness, is that "queer" has become a narrow code-word (like "heterosexism") that refers exclusively to lesbians and gay men. The queer-theory crowd — who show up in person at lesbian and gay studies conferences and, in print, in collections like Diana Fuss's *Inside/Out*[4] — talk of problematizing the relationship between hetero and homo, and of getting past the taken-for-grantedness of the structures of lesbian and gay communities. While the intention here is expansive, the effects remain limited. In her introduction to a special "Queer Theory" issue of the journal *differences*, Teresa de

Lauretis juxtaposed "queer" with "lesbian and gay" as a way of marking "a certain critical distance from the latter, by now established and often convenient, formula."[5] Her hope was that queer, as a concept, would push our thinking in ways that the "and" that joins lesbian to gay never has. The idea was that queer would force us to "problematize" our more familiar sexual categories.

De Lauretis wrote her piece in 1990. But as I write this, in 1993, only three years later, the term "queer" is already so overloaded and overdetermined that a discursively innocent deployment of it is impossible. "Queer," in general homo parlance, has taken on its own set of plural meanings, no less restricting because there are more than one of them.

As usual, the flavour of this mishmash comes from its strongest (most pungent?) ingredients. A woman who used to belong to the political group Queer Nation Toronto told me she has gay male friends who now say things like: "It'll be a good party, all the queers and lesbians will be there." Expansive politics, indeed. It seems that in the sense these men use the word — though, of course, I can't be sure — "queer" implies groovy, hip, right-on, you wouldn't want to miss it. These are all adjectives that, to them, may well be synonymous with male. It's a formulation that draws on the Queer Nation definition of "queer" as the cutting edge, the front line, be there or be left out.

The other queer stereotype that gets in the way of an expansive politics is queer as academic chic. In the United States (and, in the odd instance, in Canada), in some circles, at some universities, there is mileage to be gained from being out. This material fact seems to have inspired a look (lots of leather and very trendy: lipstick, miniskirts and well-coiffed hair for the femmes; jackets, jeans and boots for the butches; jeans, J. Crew shirts and waifish pouts for the boys, etc.), a manner of speaking (heavily soaked in post-structuralist terminology, whether you know how to use it or not) and a list of potential subject areas (sex, butch/femme, identity formation, popular culture and representations of AIDS), all of which are claimed to be very revolutionary and ground-breaking.

My sarcastic tone, while marking my frustration with this "scene," shouldn't obscure the fact that there is some good work coming out of it. Nevertheless, there is a tendency among both queer academics and queer activists — who are often the same people — to see queerness itself as synonymous with radicalness and things risqué, as in: (a) we're going to do this amazing demo, blah, blah, blah, or (b) (the academic version) she's actually going to present an analysis of such and such before her straight-laced committee, can you believe it?

In both instances, "queer" is a completely lesbian and gay term, harkening back to romantic visions of the queer as outlaw and transgressor. It's as if "queer" is addressing a contemporary need for the sense of uniqueness that many lesbians and gay men feel is part of our identity. For some of us (I count myself in here), part of the allure of coming out was the chance it gave us to live "on the margins," to avoid the banality of ordinariness. I wonder, for those of us who are white, how much of this is a response to our racial identities? Is there a part of our queerness that is an attempt to distance ourselves from other aspects of our lives where we have social power? Is queerness sometimes based in a romanticization of marginality?

If we do get something out of being "on the edge," what does it mean for the broader political project of working against heterosexism? What does it mean for queerness as the basis of an expansive, not specifically lesbian/gay, counter-hegemonic project? What does it mean for any project intent on destabilizing the heterosexual norm, shifting the balance of power from the centre to the large collectivity on the various margins?

If many of us find pleasure on the margins, playing off against the hets in the centre, can we ever expect to make big-time change? Deep down, do we even want to? Are we too invested in the homo/het divide, in our own "specialness" as sexual others, in a structure that still has a place for sexual outlaws? Is it possible to imagine "queerness" in a social system without marginality?

As the lesbian and gay movement makes more and more gains, as the mainstream looms closer to our homo lives, have we grasped on to queerness to save our selves from the vapidness of acceptance? And, frankly, who could blame us if we have.

Endnotes

1. Gayle Rubin, "The traffic in women: Notes on the political economy of sex," in *Towards an Anthropology of Women*, ed. Rayna R. Reiter (New York, Monthly Review Press, 1975), 157-210.
2. Adrienne Rich, "Compulsory heterosexuality and lesbian existence," in *Powers of Desire*, ed. Ann Snitow, Christine Stansell, and Sharon Thompson (New York, Monthly Review Press, 1983), 177-205.
3. Gary Kinsman, *The Regulation of Desire* (Montreal, Black Rose, 1987).
4. Diana Fuss, ed., *Inside/Out: Lesbian Theories, Gay Theories* (New York, Routledge, 1991).
5. Theresa de Lauretis, "Queer theory: Lesbian and gay sexualities - An introduction," *differences* (Summer 1991), iv.

bizarre women, exotic bodies & outrageous sex: or, if annie sprinkle was a black ho she wouldn't be *all* that

karen/miranda augustine

The new school of lezzie pro-sex activism has been pushed into the mainstream of queer political thought. Important as it is for women's issues to be placed at the centre, and particularly so, since lesbians generally have little emotional or financial dependence on men, throughout the bulk of sex mags, porn and the Modern Primitives trend is an unacknowledged presence of culture-vulturism dependent on racialized sex-drives of white queers.

As a queer-identified Black woman, I have felt unsatisfied by the sexual liberation rhetoric firmly anchored within lesbian and gay spaces. S/M, dyke representation, censorship, pornography, sexual fantasies: this cornucopia of women's sexual practice within the mainstream of the lesbian, gay and bisexual communities has conveniently disregarded the very complex issue of race — and where it all fits — within these discussions.

I'm not big on sexuality theories because the very things that swell my clit, when thrown into the whirlwind of lezzie political correctness, just don't figure. And depending on how strong I'm feeling, shame is often the outcome, if what's turning me on is deemed degrading to my sex by the progressive elite. Put quite simply, I don't claim definitive politics on a lot of these issues, but, I do understand what makes me wet.

I am a consumer of pornography. Het porn, that is. I have been so since the age of eleven. *Cherie*, *Penthouse*...you name it, I hoarded it. What I realized then was that Black female porn stars (like their Aboriginal, Asian, Latina, Arab and Jewish sisters) were left to the pages of fetish mags, alluding to themes of cannibalism, bestiality and slavery. What I understand now is that race is *the* distinguishing feature in determining the type of objectification a woman will encounter. (bell hooks, 1992) And believe me, the sex-libbers of the queer scene need a wake-up call: this problem is alive and well, and deeply embedded within our communities. A historical briefing on Black sexual exoticization will bring me back to my case in point.

the 411

The link between the eroticization of Black sexuality, myths surrounding "whiteness," and colonial culture is lacking in the bulk of queer sex-lib theories. In examining the supposed normality of "whiteness" and the colonial construction of Black sexuality — and more importantly, how to reconceptualize that image — a different impression of the interconnectedness of race, class, gender, sexuality, power and control emerges.

The use of Black women's bodies as fetish and "entertainment" for Europeans has its roots within the colonization of Africa. In France during the 18th and 19th centuries, the sexuality of African slaves was made an area of study by scientists, naturalists and writers. The results deemed the African woman primitive and therefore more sexually intense. Interestingly enough, these "studies" attempted to separate the African/"them" from the European/"us" — not just physically, *but through presumptions regarding moral codes* — to distort African sexual agency, and to pathologize women's sexuality on the whole. For the cult of (white) womanhood was confined to notions of purity, chastity, passivity and prudence. Black womanhood was polarized against white womanhood in the metaphoric system of female sexuality — the Black woman became closely identified with illicit sex. (Hazel V. Carby, 1987)

sarah bartmann's girlie show

The genitalia of selected African slave women — referred to as "Hottentots" — were examined in order to prove that the African woman was a primitive species who most likely copulated with apes. (Sander L. Gilman, 1985) One of the many African women placed on display, Sarah Bartmann, referred to as the "Hottentot Venus," is but one example of Black female objectification during early 19th century Europe. Her display formed one of the original icons for Black female sexuality. Bartmann was often exhibited at fashionable parties in Paris, generally wearing little clothing, to provide entertainment. To her audience, she represented deviant sexuality. (Collins, 1990) Reduced to her sexual parts, Ms. Bartmann was showcased for about five years until her death at age 25 in 1815. To add insult to injury, her genitalia were dissected and placed on display at the Musée de l'Homme in Paris, where they remain to this day.

This piece of history informs present-day notions of a "free" and "open" sexuality which relies so specifically on Black sexual interpretation.

fuck lea delaria & her big black dildo jokes

question: which is more intimidating?
(a) a man, (b) a big man, (c) a big black man
question: rough sex — who are you most likely to get it from? (a) an Asian (b) an African
question: what makes Latinos so "hot-blooded"?

In an attempt to overthrow the strictures of (white) womanhood, the onslaught of dyke-sex paraphernalia asserts itself by commodifying "otherness" within certain sexual/body practices:

- body piercing, tattoos and scarification are a part of the "Modern Primitives" (an offensive and loaded term) movement — forms of body adornment inherent within Indigenous and Eastern cultures;
- in *Leatherwomen*, a book of women's sex writings, a (straight-identified) white woman is gang-raped by one Black and two Latina women (never mind that Blacks, Latinos and First Nations form the majority of those incarcerated) who are portrayed as being sexually "deviant" and violent; and
- in *Love Bites*, a book of lez-sex photography, white dykes fuck each other with big, black dildos.

Talks regarding the representation of women in porn and erotic writings have for too long remained at the gendered level. Racism unchallenged is reflected in both het and queer smut: Black men are reduced to the size and effectiveness of their penises; while Black, Aboriginal, Asian, Latina, Arab and Jewish women are viewed as anomalies, exotic treats and fetishes. Based on stereotypical notions of what a person-of-colour's body represents, strongly impressed is that sex with one offers intense sexual pleasure unparalleled in the vanilla experience.

cross-over vanillas

Reactionaries from the queer-cracker league may claim censorship over these blatant observations because I have put forth the issue of race. And reactionaries from the pink third space may attempt to regulate how we, as queers-of-colour, should knock boots proper (read: no S/M).

Yet most needed is a level of acknowledgement and social understanding regarding the cultural specificities of sexual expression. Basic examples include how dancehall, rap and Black speech are misinterpreted in the mainstream by non-Black audiences. And how, with regard to porn and other sex-smut, the racialization of Black and Brown people is taken to the nth degree and most extreme level. Perhaps what I'm trying to express most is that a lot of the debates are presuming that we are all white, and that the confines of white-body culture apply to us all. And in this case they really don't.

Stressed is not a simple trashing of lezzie-fuck culture, but rather the limitations of a sex-lib scene stuck in the rut of racial ambivalence. What one has the right to fantasize about or sexually impress is not the issue here. The question is, *How entrenched is that sexual fantasy/practice in the myth of progressive representation and the transcendence of white patriarchal expression?*

Sources

Carby, Hazel V. *Reconstructing Womanhood: The Emergence of the Afro-American Woman Novelist.* New York: Oxford University Press, 1987.

Collins, Patricia Hill. *Black Feminist Thought: Knowledge, Consciousness, and the Politics of Empowerment.* London: Harper Collins, 1990.

Gilman, Sander L. *Difference and Pathology: Stereotypes of Sexuality, Race, and Madness.* Ithaca: Cornell University Press, 1985.

hooks, bell. *Black Looks: Race and Representation.* Boston: South End Press, 1992.

pièces de résistance

Sheila Gilhooly
barbara findlay

This piece speaks to our individual resistance to, and trans-
formation of, the experience of mental hospitals. But more
importantly, the working through of it is something we did
together. It is literally and visibly true that the strength of
our individual resistance comes from the strength of our
relationship as survivors with each other. That is what re-
sistance is.

(Sheila's voice is in sans-serif type; barbara's is in serif type.)

twenty years gone: the conversation poem for sheila
did they give you shock?

> no. not shock. drugs. my
> nipples leaked. i couldn't
> see. my tongue got thick.
> finally
> i couldn't write: paradoxical reaction

they never ever said that there were side effects never
said you might lose your memory from the shock might
hallucinate from the meds (the
first time i hallucinated i said: too much meds
they said no dear that's
what the drugs are for

and gave me more)
were you
committed?

                              "if you don't sign yourself in
                                        I'll commit you"
and they call that voluntary

                                                    you?

sometimes/i was committed. other times
(i had to work hard on those times:
i had chosen, after all) other times/
i signed myself in

                                        one time
                          i signed someone else in i
                              committed her. i said
                          (she was hallucinating getting
                                              herself
                                  arrested) i said
                          if you carry on like this i
                              will commit you
                                      and she did
                                        and i did

my parents came. and some of
my brothers & aunts & uncles. later, years later,
after i'd been on TV, they quit talking in
loud voices like i was deaf & asked me
instead what it was like, to be on TV

                                      my parents
                                      never came
                                  nor anyone else

do you still/ever/wonder
if you're crazy?

                                      all the time

                  can i see your slash marks?

the shock of forgetting/the shock of remembering

I'm not sure why it feels so important to write it all down and make sure I have the details as clear as I can get them. It doesn't matter why I need to remember — maybe some because I'm so surprised and shocked and some frightened that I did forget. I tell myself — I was having shock treatments, designed to make you forget. Shock burns things directly onto the brain by creating so much misery that the image goes and only the misery of the image is left behind after the acid bath. That's what burned that image out for me. Nothing to do with me — only to do with some thoughtless (or perhaps not so thoughtless) cruelty that uses someone's ugly and horrifying suicide as a weapon against another, namely against me.

I came back from shock and after supervised-time-in-the-day-room, it was late morning. I went to my room and over to my bed to lie down. My head always ached bad on those days and I would be confused and shambling and kind of stunned. The closet was to my left. The doors were open and as I went to fall on my bed I looked over and saw. She was hanging from the clothes rail and her eyes were all bugged out and white and her tongue was pushing out of her mouth and making her mouth this ugly protrusion that didn't even look like a mouth. Her face was all puffy and bloated-like. And the smell caught in my throat and all this shit and piss was on the floor and on her legs and her nightgown. She would often throw tantrums and refuse to dress in the morning and thus refuse to go to the dining hall. Since she was there for anorexia they would force-feed her with tubes and she would snuffle all day long and whine about how mean everyone was to her — not a very likeable woman but she did have her point of view and they weren't very nice to her.

I remember retching violently.

After that I only remember being locked in seclusion and feeling humiliated and like I had brought it all on myself and how could I be so self-centred and indulgent as to get upset when she was like dead and as one of the nurses pointed out to me it's not like we even got along.

This memory will never surprise me again. It will never haunt me with its left-over of shame and guilt for something that wasn't my fault. I always knew that the pain around that wasn't mine. But for twenty years the only way I could know that was to forget what happened. Now I know that they caused me the pain. Now I will never forget. I will remember Denise.

ancient history
i asked if i could turn out the light.
you reached over me, your breast
brushing my face, and clicked us into darkness.

relieved, i rolled over, took you in my arms,
more confident the slash marks on my
wrist
would go unseen.

i had forgotten about them, forgotten to
buy a bandage, make up a story to see myself
through the possibility that we would
end up in your bed.

as i held you i ran my mind over the
chance
that your fingers would find
what your eyes couldn't see, wondered
to myself what i would say.
i held the words in my mouth
like stones:
i cut myself

a fissure opened,
deeper, bloodier, more
painful than the cuts.

i have no explanation. no story to offer.
i have no memory. only the talisman of
some other time, recent
by the healing of the scars

which will fade

this morning i stood beside you, naked,
looking into the mirror
my arm hidden behind you in a hug.

the scars will fade.

only the fissure
                    will remain.
but i still have the knife.

What Is the Matter?

In the Matter of
A Complaint to the Ontario College of Physicians and Surgeons
Re: Donald H. Upton, M.D.

I, barbara findlay, lawyer, adjunct law professor, and LlM candidate, of 5-2023 Grant St., of the City of Vancouver, Province of British Columbia, make oath and say as follows:

1. I am the complainant herein and as such have personal knowledge of the matters hereinafter deposed to except where stated and, where so stated, I verily believe them to be true.

2. (a) I was a patient of Dr. Donald Upton from approximately October 1966 to approximately August 1968, except for the summer months May to August 1967.
   (b) In October 1966 I was seventeen years and four months old.
3. During that time I was a scholarship student in first year, and then in second year, at Queen's University, Kingston, Ontario.
4. During that time Dr. Donald Upton was a psychiatrist with the Queen's Student Health Service.
5. During the time I saw Dr. Upton he had me in psychoanalysis.
6. For the first period of several months or perhaps more than a year, I saw Dr. Upton three times a week. I saw him in the second year at least twice a week, perhaps three times a week, as I recall.
7. During approximately March 24 to approximately May 1 of 1967 I was hospitalized by Dr. Upton in the psychiatric ward of Kingston General Hospital.
8. When I returned to Queen's in the fall of 1967, Dr. Upton advised me that he had been consulted by the university as to my fitness to continue school and he had told them that I would be all right provided that I continue therapy. He communicated that to me in such a way that I believed that if I discontinued therapy with him it would jeopardize my schooling.
9. (a) While I was in psychoanalysis, I believe in the fall of 1967, Dr. Upton requested that I babysit for him and his wife. I agreed.
   (b) Dr. Upton and his wife picked me up at the student residence where I was then living, driving their station wagon. I got into the back seat with his three children. I discovered that two of his three children were deaf.

(c) Dr. Upton had not told me that two of his children were deaf.

(d) When I later asked him why he had not told me that his children were deaf he said he wanted to see how I would react.

(e) While he had me in psychotherapy, Dr. Upton told me that he thought I should make my career working with deaf children. To that end he told me he wanted to introduce me to a friend of his who worked with deaf children in Belleville, Ontario. However, though he carried the idea and the promise in front of me, the meeting never happened.

1O. (a) During the summer of 1968 Dr. Upton hired me and another of his patients, a male student, to work on a project for the summer.

(b) The project was to do research and a survey related to the ability or lack thereof of women students successfully to perform in engineering schools. The hypothesis was that women were unable successfully to do engineering because of an inability to conceptualize spatially.

(c) I was to be paid $1000 for the work over the summer.

(d) The other student and I were assigned reading to do, and left to work together. Dr. Upton asked me during therapy how I was getting along with the male student, and suggested to me that I should draw him out. He said that this student was very shy, and was also a scholarship student, and it would be therapeutic for him if I drew him out. I later discovered that he had told the male student the same thing about me.

(e) Dr. Upton never paid me any money at all for the work of the summer. When I asked him in September 1968 about being paid, he said he was not going to pay me. I do not remember his explanation.

11. On one occasion while I was in therapy with Dr. Upton, he told me something about his life of which he was ashamed. He told me that if I ever repeated what he said he would deny having said it.

12. During the entire time that I was in psychoanalysis with Dr. Upton I believed that I was seriously mentally ill and that my only hope of redemption lay through working with him.

13. I remember very little of the content of the psychoanalysis that I did with Dr. Upton.

14. I am a lesbian. I discovered that I might be a lesbian at the time I was in psychoanalysis with Dr. Upton. He refused to acknowledge the possibility.

15. I have been treated subsequently by psychiatrists and by lay therapists. I was hospitalized for six weeks in 1968.

16. I have not made a complaint about the treatment I received from Dr. Upton before now because it was not until I was relating my psychiatric history recently that I realized that his behaviour was professionally inappropriate.

17. This affidavit is sworn to the best of my information, belief, and recollection.

18. I swear this affidavit is in support of a formal complaint to the College of Physicians and Surgeons of Ontario with respect to the conduct of Dr. Donald Upton as herein described and sworn.

Sworn before me this _____ day of _____ 1991 at the City of Vancouver, Province of British Columbia.

_____   _____
A Commissioner for taking Oaths in   barbara findlay
the Province of British Columbia

dear shari

well, old friend, i'm at it again.

here it is, 26 November 1991 2:20 am, writing away in a hot blaze of anger and pain. i have just written a four-page affidavit so that i can swear a formal complaint against dr. upton, that shrink i saw yea, these many years ago. remember him? he's the one that put me in the hospital that first time, when you were in alliston and i was in kingston.

this summer i went off to see if i was (still? again?) crazy. i didn't tell you at the time since you were on your way to australia for the fall and i didn't want to weigh you down with worry (are you mad? don't be). the expedition was a complete and utter waste of time as the psychiatrist behaved just like a psychiatrist — she said, when i asked her what benefit she thought i would get and how long she thought this would take, that she wondered why i wanted to know that. because i don't take my car in for repair without knowing that sort of thing, i said. and what kind of work did she do? i went on. as in, whose work did she value. well, she said, i could tell you that but i don't think it would be appropriate. it is clear that you have an issue about control, she continued.

no kidding. i couldn't believe it. it was out of a 1950 parody of psychiatry.

however, it was in the course of relating the treatment i'd had from upton (and her response, which was that it was abusive) that i suddenly realized how awful it all was.

(and if i am still crazy, well, i am still crazy. i take comfort in the thought that i am also the sanest person i know.)

so here i am, months later and in the middle of the night (at this rate of processing things i'll still be up at 3 a.m. when i'm 102) FURIOUS. i think of myself: a CHILD, for christs sake. and the way he treated me!!! he would have been about the age i am now. i can't imagine treating a teenager, a teenager completely dependent on me and absolutely trusting of me, like that.

i don't think i can convey the depth of my rage, which is deeper than deep because it has taken so long for me to see that what he did was wrong.

i really hope that i don't discover that he abused me in ways i don't yet remember. i couldn't possibly handle that much anger.

i have had many kickbacks of self-blame as i composed my dry affidavit: this is no big deal. lots of people had it worse than you. what are you whining about? it's your fault anyway — you dingbat, why didn't you raise a stink at the time if he didn't pay you for the work he hired you to do? what a fool. no one is going to believe you now anyway. you know your memory is the pits — how can you be so absolutely sure of these things (and i am) if you can't remember any of the rest of it? if you tell them this they will just discredit you as a pervert/sick/whatever (i put it all in the affidavit — being a lesbian, having subsequent treatment — say everything, they can't get you on nothing, then).

what good is it going to do now, anyway?

my mind races to a cross-examination:

now, ms findlay, you say you have had extensive shall we say emotional or mental treatment over the years?

i have seen therapists, yes.

could you detail, please, for the court, who you saw, for how long, and for what purpose?

OBJECTION, my lord. the issue in this case is, first, whether the defendant did or did not do what the complainant ms findlay alleges, and second, if he did, whether the conduct contravenes the ethical standards of the college. i

fail to see how questioning the complainant about her inter-
vening treatment goes to either of those questions.

with the greatest of respect to my learned friend (they
always say this when they're being sarcastic) she continues
to miss the point she is making. <u>of course</u> the issue is
whether my client did or did not do something twenty-three
years ago. if he did not, then there must be a reason that the
complainant says that he did. perhaps she believes he did
but is deluded (shades of anita hill — did you get that story
down there?). perhaps she has had the idea suggested to her
by her latest psychiatrist. perhaps her memory is selective,
or partial, or simply mistaken. i want to explore all of those
possibilities and i submit i have the right and the duty on
behalf of my client to canvass each and every one of those
possibilities with the utmost thoroughness. if a professional
is to be held to account for actions or inactions past the time
of any limitation act for civil action, if we as a society are to
conclude that the professional's liability extends that far,
and that he or she may be disciplined or even lose his or her
licence on the basis of allegations that are this old, then
surely we must be scrupulous about permitting the defendant in that situation every latitude in cross-examination.

my lord, this is one of those cases, like rape cases, like
sexual harassment cases, where the conduct of the case itself
is as important to the outcome as substance of the com-
plaint. if you permit my learned friend limitless cross-ex-
amination, in effect requiring the complainant to reveal all
of her personal history for the past twenty-three years, as a
condition of a successful prosecution, then the message you
will be sending to all patients who may have been or may
be mistreated by their physicians is that the price of com-
plaining is far too high. there must be a balance.

once again, my lord, my friend has tripped over her own

point. we had a rape shield law. presumably it was enacted out of the very sentiments the crown refers to. it protected rape victims from cross-examination about their prior sexual history. but, my lord, as you will be aware, that law was struck down only a few months ago in the *seaboyer* case. so much as i appreciate the concerns of my learned friend on behalf of the complainant, and indeed much as i sympathize with the situation of any complainant in proceedings such as these, in my respectful submission the law cannot substitute sympathy for justice.

the judge: i have your objection, madame crown counsel, and argument from both of you. i shall take time to consider my ruling. court stands adjourned till tomorrow morning.

etc. etc. etc. etc. etc. (in whose favour would YOU rule??? actually i think the crown isn't a very good lawyer. i imagine a young woman, maybe five years experience, up against some high-priced senior grey-haired male litigator...)

fortunately i recognize the self-blame kickbacks for what they are — but it makes it only marginally easier. fuck it is hard and fuck it is infuriating and fuck it is unfair to have to live my life in the face of a global expectation that i will not be believed. it occurs to me that that is why i am so honest most of the time!!! they don't believe me even when i tell the truth, they'll NEVER believe me if i lie.

anyway. my stomach is churning, my jaws are clenched and i can see sleep will be a while to come yet. fortunately for me i just happen to have 100 or 200 hours of work here, so no problem. and i don't have to get up in the morning.

to the "why bother" question, which is the one that keeps recurring, the answer seems to be: i have all these credibility papers for something. i have a responsibility to use them. in other words if *i'm* afraid they won't believe *me* — socially certified credible as i am, what with all these degrees — who WILL they believe? and who COULD have the courage.

anyway. it's now 26 November 1991 3:03 a.m. writing that little cross-examination has amused me and brought my rage level down to manageable proportions. i'm actually feeling sleepy.

take care. love to both of you.

barbara

p.s. 26 November 1991 9:43 a.m.

i phoned the ontario college of physicians and surgeons to file the complaint.

donald howard upton died a year ago.

November 28,1991

Dear barbara

I told you I would remember how it went so I'm writing it all down before going to sleep in case anything gets lost before morning. Then I can tell you about it if you forget, and you can also have your own record.

So it went like this. You read me the affidavit, the cross-examination, the letter to Shari — all about Dr. Upton. I asked you how it felt to have all the details clear and remembered. You said you felt bad but that it all seemed very puny to you and maybe you were just whining about something that wasn't so terrible. (you, who are so *not* like that. it's amazing how they make us question even the things that are most true about ourselves) I said I didn't think it was puny, you asked me to say more about that — so I did. I said I thought he had used you and abused your trust and cheated you, and all the while claiming to be the only thing standing between you and madness. You said, "I could have said something about it then." I reminded you that you were seventeen years old and dependent on this man and he manipulated you. We

62

talked about how being manipulated left one feeling like "maybe it was all my fault," and we talked about how much shame went with that. Then I'm pretty sure I said "he should be ashamed, not you." You then said DON'T SAY THAT most emphatically. I asked what part, and you kept repeating "don't say that" and sounding more and more distressed each time. Your breathing got faster and very laboured. I asked again what not to say and you said something about shame that I didn't catch, and your breathing got really raw. Then you said "it hurts" with such anguish that the words seemed to be squeezed out of you. You asked me to talk to you and I did and all the while you struggled painfully to breathe. You cried out in pain and you said several times that it hurt too much. I kept talking and you kept breathing like that for some time and you said NO with great distress many, many times. After a while, your breathing started coming back to normal and I said your name and you said "I'm okay really I am" and then you asked me what was happening with me. I talked a bit about that but was more interested at that moment in what was going on for you. But before I could ask, you asked me what had just happened, and said you couldn't remember any of it. So I told you all this as well as I could remember the exact order of things. You had no memory of it and were trying to figure out when and why you left the conversation. We talked about shame as we had been talking before the pain started. You stated again that you could have protested back then (though I don't see how) and that he could have done worse and you were pretty sure he hadn't. You said nobody would think it was a big deal, or even believe it ever happened. I told you I believed you, and that it felt to me like a very big deal. You asked me what I was feeling and I said very tender about you and very angry at him for what he did to you, for all those details set out in the affidavit, and I started to review them and then you said "he did worse." I asked you to tell me about it and you made a couple of starts and then your breathing started to go very raw again. You cried out in great pain and kept saying — "no, don't do this." This time it was shorter but seemed more painful and much more fearful. Breathing seemed to hurt just as much but when you said NO it seemed more about another fear than the pain. The first time had seemed all about the pain or at least that's all you spoke of. You didn't say so much this time except no but I could feel the terror in your voice and that terror was real. Again your breathing went slowly back to normal, and again you asked me what was going on for me. You didn't accept "I'm fine," so I elaborated some and kind of made my way back to what you had said about Dr. Upton doing worse. You told me you had no words left and that you wouldn't remember any of it. I told you I would remember it for you. You apologized for whimpering at me and I told you that you never had to be sorry for that. You thanked me for being there for you. I tell you again and as many times as you want to hear it — I'm right here, I'm not going anywhere. I have a strong stomach, I'm not afraid and I love you very much.

Sheila

Who's That Teacher? The Problems of Being a Lesbian Teacher of Colour

Diane Williams

As the late Jim Henson's Kermit the Frog sang, "It ain't easy bein' green." It ain't easy bein' a Black lesbian schoolteacher, either. Teachers who are both homosexual and of colour face pressures in the classroom from many storm fronts.

That pressure can be internal, as the teacher attempts to define herself as a member of several groups that operate outside of, and often in spite of, the white male heterosexual culture.

That pressure can be recognizably external, as the teacher attempts to assume her responsibility to society, to the students, and to herself, which includes all of her "folks" (Black, lesbian, feminist, etc.).

This external pressure can be administrative as the teacher is encouraged to expand the experiences of her students — as long as that expansion is not too provocative or threatening to these frequently indifferent but fertile young minds.

So, how does this hip young educator battle a system that — like the 300-pound gorilla whose sheer weight and demeanour allows him to sit anywhere he pleases — is designed to be immovable in its definition of what is appropriate and normal? She does so with teeth and fists clenched.

Defining myself as a Black person, as a woman and as a Black woman — three separate and sometimes unequal roles — is the easiest task in a classroom. No matter what kind of campus I am on — college or adult education, black or white — my colour and gender are apparent before I say "Good morning" on the first day of class. If students have built-in stereotypes of what I should be — ignorant in some cases, elitist in others — I can peel those away slowly with appropriate references to William Shakespeare, John Steinbeck, James Joyce, James Baldwin, Malcolm X and Gwendolyn Brooks.

Defining my lower middle-class background is also important. I do not want my urban students to think I have become one of *them* — whatever they define THEM as at the moment — and I do not want my students on the green suburban campuses to think that I have forgotten the significance of my even being behind a podium there. Elitism is not on my already crowded agenda.

This crowded agenda includes responsibility to the student as a member of society and as a member of an educational system. What greater good can I do in a classroom than by expressing my Blackness, rather than ignoring it, or by letting my lavender cloak peep from my closet? Perhaps my students will be able to — for a brief period — realize that THOSE PEOPLE they've been so leery of are not that much different from who they now believe themselves to be. If they understand this for that academic moment, they *might* — just might — treat the next "different" person they come across with more equanimity. They might think before they use words like *nigger* or *faggot* so freely. They might — or they might just earn their credit, and my presence will be no more than that of an apparition encountered on their way to a diploma or a degree.

How does this apparition hope to have a lasting effect? By incorporating my responsibilities to myself into my lesson plans. I can — with administrative approval, of course — slip in books that will make my students think beyond the questions of literary mechanisms. I can slip in works that express the universality of human experience as well as the uniqueness of belonging to groups that champion individuality out of necessity.

I can offer my students, without disturbing their worlds too much or too quickly, the down-home power that Alice Walker's Shug Avery held over Celie in *The Color Purple*. I can discuss the stereotyped yet vivid portrayal of "The Two" in Gloria Naylor's *The Women of Brewster Place*. I can read them the poetry of Audre Lorde and the drama of Ntozake Shange. I can answer literary questions as honestly as possible without offering too many shifts in pronouns from *she* to the obligatory *he*. I can carry pride in all my identities by posing for thought the intimate relationship of D.H. Lawrence's Banford and March in *The Fox* or the feverish relationship of the strong Theodora and the timid Eleanor in Shirley Jackson's *The Haunting of Hill House*.

Sometimes these small unexpected doses of difference go down much easier than works that demand to be recognized as gay or lesbian, including my own prose and poetry. In small, already overheated classrooms, a work that explores the love without speaking its name seeps through the cracks of these young walls built of -isms — racism, heterosexism, and classism (we won't even get into the ongoing struggle to conquer looksism) — and that becomes a welcome victory in this battle against growing intolerance.

I know that these victories are few and precious because

I have taught on a 95 per cent white campus in the Chicago suburb of Des Plaines where much of the faculty, staff and student body seem content to play the Assimilation Game. For example, while I was happy to be on campus representing some sense of cultural and sexual self-worth, I heard a South Asian student assistant ask her blonde counterpart if the Indian student's accent were noticeable.

"Can you tell," she asked, biting her bottom lip in sincerity, "that I am from India?" This did not seem to bother anyone else in the office, but I quickly added Toni Morrison and Cheryl Clarke to my reading list in an effort to chip away harder at these internalized -isms.

I also have taught at urban sites, and the students there have the same problem of ghettoization that suburban students have: WE are the world, so those OTHER FOLKS must be alien. Once, a student announced in one of my adult education classes that he quit his job because "There are too many faggots working down there." I wanted to rip open my shirt to reveal that lavender L beneath it, but — like Superman's alter ego Clark Kent — I recognize the need for some surreptitiousness. Alienating the adult-education population on Chicago's West Side would only fuel the fires of intolerance or — worse — indifference. I simply reminded him in that firm, teacherly way that what he said was no more acceptable than calling someone a nigger, that the world contains a variety of people, and that those people — peek-a-boo — are everywhere. He mumbled something inaudible and dropped it. In time, I thought, like drops of rain pounding a rock, I could erode this wall of self-hatred and outward hostility.

This is why I choose to continue to fight in the bowels of the system. In an ideal world I could be absolutely open everywhere, with no fear that I would turn off my students before I could turn them on to the larger world around them. Instead, in this often cruel landscape, I try to be all things — a good teacher, a strong Black woman, an unashamed lesbian and a decent human being — and in spite of not having all of these hats always fit comfortably when worn together, I try not to give up my internal sense of Self while battling external pressures in the classroom. I cannot afford to give up my identity while trying to help students find some deeper meaning in themselves.

No, it ain't easy bein' Black and lavender in a room full of students who come in wearing their preconceived notions like boxing gloves and with their defense mechanisms charged up, but as the only representative of real difference that many of them have ever had, I cannot give up or unclench my own literary fists. I owe it to mySelf, and to my "folks."

Lesbian Parenting: Cracking the Shell of the Nuclear Family

Rachel Epstein

On June 9, 1994 I was on the steps of the Ontario legislature with my two-year-old daughter when Bill 167 (the equality-rights bill for lesbian and gay families) was defeated. Although I had been only peripherally involved in the organizing leading up to the bill, its defeat was like a kick in the stomach. I held my daughter as she first hesitantly, then joyously, copied the clenched-fisted crowd yelling "Shame! Shame!" Latex-gloved police officers pushed us with riot sticks down the legislature stairs to the outside. We had just been wiped off the personhood map, given a loud, clear message that we are *not* legitimate people, deserving of the same rights and privileges as anyone else.

It's not that Bill 167 was the answer to all our problems. In fact, the reaction to the bill shows how big our problems really are. The hatred and homophobia unleashed by the proposal that lesbians and gays have equal rights were astounding. Singled out as particularly immoral and disgusting were the ideas that lesbians and gays could adopt children and that lesbian and gay people who already have children be considered "families."

Images come to my mind:

- My daughter, Sadie, is born at home surrounded by a loving and cheering network of eight lesbian aunties, two lesbian midwives and two lesbian moms. Many of these people become an extended family to Sadie, providing her with love, fun and stimulation, and her moms with a break.
- Sadie figures out that she has two moms. "Sadie have two mommies. I hug them," she says, as she grabs our necks.
- My partner and I and Sadie are boarding a plane to Vancouver. The woman who is checking us in turns to me with a big smile and says, "It's so nice traveling with help, isn't it?"
- Our close friends, Sadie's doting other family, have been trying for years to get pregnant. Now they want to adopt. The one who will officially adopt is told by a social worker "You're Jewish and you're lesbian, that's two strikes against you."

One of the arguments used to support Bill 167 is that lesbian and gay families are "just like" heterosexual, "normal" families. In many ways we are. We often live as couples, have children, work, take care of the kids, worry about schools, child-rearing, money, etc. But we are different, too. Our very existence poses a fundamental challenge to the traditional model of the nuclear family, a model which defines parenting roles through biology. The existence of lesbian families points to the need for redefinition of "parent" and "family."

When I was six months pregnant, I interviewed three other co-parenting lesbian couples. The baby felt imminent. I wanted to know how lesbians who were parenting in couples were defining and living out their parenting roles and, in so doing, how they were challenging and/or supporting the traditional family model. Conducting these interviews was rich and inspiring. I sat in living rooms and kitchens, and asked questions that were immediately relevant to my own life, and then theorized about the answers and their larger implications for our lives as lesbians. The women I interviewed were ''ordinary'' lesbians like myself. I found in their words a reminder of the courage it takes to lead one's life in contradiction to the dominant society, and an inspiration in their thoughtfulness, self-awareness and insistence on being who they are. While parenting small children sometimes results in a withdrawal from active political life, the issues raised by lesbian parenting puts us right in the middle of theoretical and strategic debates currently being waged in the lesbian and gay movement, and in the larger political arena, as well.

Lesbians Choosing Children

North America is experiencing a lesbian baby boom. More and more lesbians are choosing, *as lesbians*, to become parents. Lesbian parenting in itself is not a new phenomenon. Lesbians have always parented children, but usually in the context of heterosexual marriages or relationships. Over the past approximately fifteen years, lesbians in increasing numbers are choosing either to give birth or to adopt children in the context of their identity as lesbians. While statistics are virtually impossible to come by, the numbers are clearly in the thousands.[1]

A lesbian who chooses to have a child faces myriad of issues and decisions. She needs to decide whether she wants to adopt, or to get pregnant and give birth. If she is trying to biologically bear a child, she must choose either alternative insemination or sexual relations with a man as a means to get pregnant. If she opts for the first choice, she has to weigh the pros and cons of a known versus an unknown sperm donor; and she has to decide what criteria are important to her when selecting donors and what legal or other arrangements she wants to make with the donor.

She also has to make her decision about the organization of the family she wants to parent within. Some lesbians are choosing to be single parents, some are co-parenting in couples, and others are developing more innovative parenting models. These include inclusion of a known sperm donor as a parent figure or co-parenting with one or more lesbians or gay men.

This article looks particularly at the parenting roles being developed by lesbians who are co-parenting in couples. I am a thirty-eight-year-old white, Jewish, middle-class lesbian mother. I am co-parenting a baby girl with my partner of seven years. I am the biological parent; she, the non-biological. As we raise our daughter, we engage in an ongoing process of defining our different roles in relationship to our child. We have few models for a family with two female parents; we develop them ourselves through experience, observation and sharing of information with other lesbian families.

My partner's view is influenced by her experience in a previous lesbian relationship, in which the other woman gave birth to a son, whom they co-parented as two mothers, until they separated when he was two years old. They continued to co-parent from separate residences until the other woman decided she didn't want to co-parent any more and denied my partner access to the child. After a long and painful process, the child is now back in my partner's life every second weekend. This experience has caused her to think deeply about the implications of the "two mothers" definition and the realities in terms of power and control that exist in each "mother" role. I, too, have been heavily influenced by watching this experience and seeing the pain involved.

I did this research because I wanted to learn about the parenting models people had developed within the families they were creating. I wanted to know about the possibilities of developing egalitarian parenting roles that acknowledge the differences between "mothers," that are not based on the premise that both parents will play *exactly* the same role(s), and that protect the rights and feelings of the non-biological parent. And I wanted to examine the forces in society and within ourselves that hinder us in our creation of family.

The women I interviewed were asked their age, how long they had identified themselves as lesbians, the ages and birth mothers of their child(ren), and their class/racial/cultural background. With their names changed, they are:

Couple 1:   Anne - 35 years old, lesbian for 17 years, middle class, Scottish Protestant (WASP), biological mother to Marie, age 5, non-biological mother to Karl, age 7.

Barb - 31 years old, lesbian for 10 years, working class, white, assimilated francophone, biological mother to Karl, age 7, non-biological mother to Marie, age 5.

Barb gave birth to Karl, their first child; they were both at home for four months, then Barb went back to work. Anne got pregnant when Karl was eight months old and was home with both children for two and a half years.

Couple 2:   Chris - 38 years old, lesbian for 15 years, middle class, white, (WASP), biological mother to Trudie, age 5.

Deb - 50 years old, lesbian for 15 years, middle class, African/English/French/Portuguese Jew, grew up in Jamaica until age 19, non-biological mother to Trudie, age 5.

Chris gave birth to Trudie, their only child. She was at home for nine months, and then went back to work. Deb returned to work when Trudie was six weeks old, then at nine months was at home for one year, and then went back to work part-time.

Couple 3:   Eli - 29 years old, lesbian for 15 years, working class, culturally Canadian, racially African, grew up in Barbados, biological mother to Lila, age 1, non-biological mother to Elvira, age 2.

Fay - 31 years old, lesbian for 11 years, working class, South Asian Black, grew up in Jamaica, biological mother to Elvira, age 2, non-biological mother to Lila, age 1.

Fay gave birth to Elvira, their first child. They were both at home for six months, then Fay went back to work. Eli got pregnant when Elvira was one month old, and is now at home with both children.

Challenging the Nuclear Family

When I refer to the traditional model of the nuclear family, I am referring to a model which consists of a heterosexual married couple with one or more children who are genetically related to the parents. The woman and children are economically dependent on the man: he is the primary breadwinner; she, the primary caretaker of physical and emotional needs. The children are the property of the parents, and the parents have authority over the children. All of these roles are considered "natural." This is the ideological model upon which most social policies related to the family is based; it does not necessarily describe what North American families actually look like.

The existence of lesbian couples who insist on their right to have children together and on the non-biological parent's role as a mother, challenges the family model based on heterosexuality, marriage and biologically related children. Lesbian families also challenge the male-female roles prescribed by the traditional model and offer alternative visions of parenting roles and division of labour within a family.

Division of Labour

The division of labour within lesbian households (i.e., who stays home with children, who goes to work) is not based on the presumed economic dependence of a woman on a man, but rather on which partner can get work, who can make more money and what each partner desires. All the women I interviewed described a similar negotiation process leading to decisions about who would work at home and who would go out to work.

> A lot of those decisions came from Eli. She put out that she would like to stay home. I was fine with that because I wanted to go back to work. I know with having children how expensive it is and I wanted the children to have more choices.   Fay

…it was always going to be 50-50 in terms of who did the work. Who went out and had a job would depend on what opportunities came up for us.　　　Deb

These decisions are not always easy to make and each location (at home, in the workforce) brings with it different fears, feelings and resentments.

I won't sit here and say there's no resentment, of course there is. I mean you've (she indicates her partner) talked to real grown-up people all day, that actually have opinions and feelings. And then she turns around and says to me, 'But you watched Elvira walk first and you listened to her first whatever'…so trying not to get the 'grass is greener' syndrome, realizing there are many flaws being out there and there are many flaws being in here.　　　Eli

What differentiates these couples from what might be the common experience of heterosexual couples is their *flexibility* in terms of who does what. If one partner expresses distress about the work she is doing, there is room for negotiation and change.

I clearly remember the day when I said to Barb 'The flags are starting to fly, Barb, I gotta get out of here. I've talked baby babble for a year and a half now, I don't know what it's like to socialize with adults, I've got to get out.' *So that was the end of that phase.* (Emphasis mine.)　　　Anne

Names

What the child(ren) would call each parent was an issue for each couple. Most wanted names that implied some form of equality between the parents, and some definitely wanted to be called some form of ''mommyism.''

> We figured whatever it was, it would be something that was equal, so when she first started talking she'd call us 'Mama Chris' and 'Mama Deb,' and then she just dropped the 'Mama' at some point and she uses our first names now. She's always referred to both of us as her mom, or 'my moms.'   Deb

> We both wanted some form of mommyism, and not first names. I ended up believing in the theory that the kids would pick for themselves. And now they do. And they have different names for different situations. It's like 'Mom-m-m' does a certain job, and 'Where's Anne!' does another, but mostly it's 'Mommy Anne' and 'Mama Barb' They went through a long period of just calling us by our first names. I would say, 'Won't you call me Mom sometimes, or Mommy Anne? All my life I wanted to have a kid partly so somebody would call me Mom.' So later on when they feel like they're being really nice and generous to me they say, 'Don't you notice I'm calling you Mom more often?'   Anne

The child's last name is always an issue because a hyphenated name made up of the surnames of two women is not legally recognized.

> Elvira has my last name which worked out quite strangely because there was a father part you're sup-

posed to fill out on the form from City Hall. I filled it
out, and Fay brought it back. My first name could be
male or female so they didn't say anything. So Elvira's
last name is a hyphenated form of both our names. Legally, of course, that doesn't stand up, 'cause we're not
legal people.   Eli

Parenting Roles

Contrary to the gender-prescribed roles explicit in the traditional model, lesbian parenting roles are based on each
woman's personality, likes and dislikes, and style. One parent may be the "funny" parent, the other more serious; one
does sports with the kids, the other pushes academics; one
is more easygoing, the other more hard line; one does out-
door activities, the other is a homebody and cooks and sews
with the kids; one does shopping, the other art work; one is
very playful with the kids, the other stresses practical things
like storytelling and reading; one does more communication
and emotional caretaking, the other teaches technical skills
like guitar-playing and how to use tools. The challenge to
gender-defined roles is profound. As Deb said, "We're not
modelling male-female power dynamics, we're modelling
women doing everything that needs to be done in order to
maintain life. So I think it's very different."

One of the significant things that emerged in the discussions about roles was the feelings associated with being the
non-biological parent. Feelings of being excluded can hit the
non-biological lesbian mother, even before the baby is born.
A non-biological lesbian mother, unlike a father in a heterosexual relationship, doesn't have a defined role in helping
her partner get pregnant.

79

> Anne was really feeling like 'I want to be the one to get you pregnant. I want to have a role in this.' But she didn't have that role and that was really hard for her.   Barb

All of the women I interviewed acknowledged that the period of breast-feeding was the period where the difference between the biological and non-biological parent was most marked. A breast-feeding infant is much more dependent on and tied to its biological mother than on anyone else. Nobody else can meet her/his physiological or nurturing needs as fully. This almost always results in some feelings of jealousy and being left out on the part of the non-biological parent.

> From the day she was born Marie hated the bottle. So Anne was tied to her. This caused conflict between Anne and I because I could not comfort Marie. I wanted to feed her. It caused conflict, too, between me and Marie at times because I'd think 'Does she love me?'   Barb

> I think Eli felt left out because if I had to go away for an hour or so, she couldn't feed her because she was on the breast; so there was a sense of 'There's nothing I can do for you.'   Fay

The feeling of being left out of breast-feeding seems to be compensated for if the non-biological mother becomes the "at home" parent and spends more time with the kid(s).

> At four months she stopped breast-feeding and went to her new job and I was the full-time at-home mom. So

whatever bonding stuff around breast-feeding I might
have been worried about was obviously easily compensated for by the fact that I was doing hours and hours
with them.   Anne

...they would end up being closer to me because I'm at
home most of the time so I spend all the awake time
with them. Elvira (non-biological daughter) gets up in
the morning and zoom she's in the bedroom talking to
me.   Eli

In the case where the couple had only one child, it
seemed to take longer for the relationships to equalize, even
when the non-biological mother spent lots of time as the
primary caretaker.

I knew she would be more attached to Chris because of
breast-feeding. It didn't matter when she was a little
baby, it mattered later on when she was able to clearly
show a preference, which she did. If she got hurt and
we were both there, she'd go to Chris first, or she'd
want Chris at night. Now she's five and that has evened
out, but fairly recently.   Deb

Some biological mothers spoke about their desire to have
their partner bond with the baby in order to share the
emotional responsibility.

I didn't want any sort of ownership. Yes, this is my
birth child, but I want you to bond with whoever you
want to bond with, because otherwise for me it becomes
a lot of emotional responsibility and a lot of stuff on me
and me alone. The reality is, there will come a point

when you have your life and I have my life, and if I haven't learned to let go, it becomes harder the older I get. So it was important for me, for the two of them to establish how they will operate with each other.   Fay

One choice the lesbian non-biological parent has that fathers share, but rarely exercise, is the option to actually suckle the babies they didn't give birth to. While it can take a great deal of effort to actually produce milk, suckling for comfort is easy to do.

> I suckled my first born for the first month and a half.
> Comfort suckling they call it. Instead of using a pacifier
> she would do that.   Eli

Non-biological parents also spoke about the insecurity of their parenting role and, indirectly, about the power of the biological parent. Because non-biological lesbian parents are not legally recognized or socially sanctioned, their "right" to mother can be "granted" or taken away by the birth mother.

> I remember when Karl was about 24 hours old, me saying to Barb 'You better be absolutely sure that you agree with what we said all along, cause I'm hooked... If you don't see me quite the same as a mother, you tell me right away, because if you tell me that a week from now, we have a large battle on our hands, 'cause you'll be fighting with his mom, not just with your lover, but with his mom.'   Anne

> When Marie was born we had a hard time because I was sure Anne didn't love Karl as much any more cause

she had her own biological baby. I had to ask 'Does this all still make sense to you? Does this relationship mean something to you? Are we really a family unit or are we a mother and a child and a mother and a child?'...

Another difference is that her relationship with the baby is there from the day of conception. Mine is there, too, but external, and doesn't really begin until the moment of her birth. So I felt nine months behind.   Barb

Homophobia and Heterosexism: Undermining the Challenge

Institutionalized homophobia and heterosexism embedded in the society and encountered in the behaviours of family, friends and institutions undermine lesbian families.

Family: "My daughter's friend's daughter"

All the women I interviewed spoke about ongoing struggles with family members, particularly parents, to get them to recognize the legitimacy of the non-biological parent and to consider themselves grandparents to the children their daughter's partners gave birth to. This struggle for recognition can have a history in the family's refusal to recognize or accept the initial lesbian relationship, let alone the children that become a part of it. "My daughter's friend's daughter" is how one lesbian's mother described the child her daughter is parenting but didn't give birth to. This description sums up her refusal to legitimate her daughter's primary relationship and role as a parent. Another woman described being referred to, in a joking manner, by her partner's family as the "aunt" or "live-in nanny."

> Her family didn't acknowledge our relationship. I
> would always be introduced as Chris' friend, or *our*
> friend even, but nothing real. But you understand that,
> you live with that. It became more of a personal issue
> when there was a kid there and I got referred to as the
> aunt or the live-in nanny. It would be sort of a joke, just
> to deal with her own discomfort I expect.   Deb

The homophobic behaviours of family members range from extreme acts of exclusion, almost akin to "disowning," to much more subtle forms of showing preference for biological links — taking one kid out but not the other, forgetting a birthday, writing to one but not the other, refusing to recognize a non-biological grandchild in public.

Lack of legal protection for non-biological lesbian parents means that negative reactions from parents can lead to fears about claims they might make on the grandchildren, if anything happens to the children's parents, particularly to the biological parent. Women talked about the need to get parents to sign a written statement agreeing not to make such a claim because, as Anne said, "You know when people die, people get weird. So really we should do it."

Rejection by the biological family is a contributing factor in the establishment by many lesbians of what might be called an "extended family by choice" — a supportive network of people who act as family to one another. By establishing family ties that are *not based on biology*, lesbians once again challenge traditional notions of family.

> I'm not a nuclear family because I have many extended
> people, many extensions in my family. I know that our
> children will be able to turn to many people in our com-

munity because we have established the bonds for
them.   Eli

Friends: ''How can a kid have two moms?''

Although it is less frequent and less threatening, lesbian
parents also run into confusion and homophobia from peers
who do not understand or accept the family forms they are
creating. Sometimes, friends just can't get their head around
the concept of two women parenting together and will only
confer true ''mother'' status on the biological parent.

> When I talk about Elvira being my daughter my
> straight friends say 'But no, she's Fay's daughter.' They
> have to make it very clear that she's Fay's biological
> daughter.   Eli

> The ones who stand out are the friends who said 'Oh,
> Anne, you're going to be a father.' And I was just ready
> to prove them right by slugging them in the jaw. I think
> it was a big admission of their own confusion and ho-
> mophobia about roles. How could I be a mom, how can
> a kid have two moms? This might be someone who
> claims to be the most radical lesbian on earth, but when
> she's faced with this reality she doesn't know what to
> do with it.   Anne

Within the lesbian community, lesbian parents, and particularly women who identify as or are seen to be butch, run
into stereotypes and expectations about butch/femme roles.

> Because I'm the butch and Barb's the femme, it scared
> them. Not too much questioning or doubting about
> Barb and her role and how she'd handle it. She wears a

skirt, she gives birth, fine, great. She's got tits, she'll breast-feed, no problem. But what's Anne going to do? Even more so when I was pregnant. That was hard on me, being a pregnant butch.   Anne

 When I was breast-feeding my daughter at a memorial for a friend, I did what I always do and whipped out my breast and decided to feed my little girl. Three women commented about it, that they never thought they'd see me breast-feeding. It sort of struck me as 'But why, I'm female and I have a child and of course I'm going to breast-feed.' But just that stringency that's adhered to by sort of 'walk tall and proud' butches. I guess I call myself a new age butch.   Lila

Institutions: "Talk to me like I'm his mom"

Lesbian parents, like all parents, have to deal with institutions such as hospitals, day cares and schools. This means having to make choices about how and with whom to be "out" and when to intervene on behalf of your kids.

All the women I interviewed had chosen to be very "out" in dealing with institutions in order to instil confidence, not fear, in their children.

Oh, everybody knows that we're two moms. We've always been open. Our feeling is that we're much safer being out than being in the closet. Because we'd be acting like we had something to hide and that message comes across to our kids, like 'don't talk about this or don't talk about that.' I don't want to instil any fear. I want my kids to be confident in who they are and in our family, and that means that we have to be, too.   Barb

But being "out" means encountering and dealing with homophobic responses which again can vary in their intensity, from extremely serious to mildly annoying. Non-biological parents are sometimes refused admission to parent-teacher interviews, or are denied permission to make important medical decisions for their children if the biological parent is not present. And then there is the day-to-day unpleasantness of people's reactions to a lesbian family.

> You can tell a doctor three times 'Talk to me like I'm his mother, so is she...' and they don't get it. Sometimes, they really say, 'I don't know what you're talking about.' 'We're two lesbians, we're both the mother.' 'Huh. No, I'll talk to the one with the dress, that's safe.'   Anne

Schools are a major institution that lesbian mothers have to confront. Many of the women I interviewed have had positive experiences with individual teachers, although they also talked about their parenting status being tolerated but not acknowledged in the classroom.

Kids of lesbians have to learn to deal with homophobic reactions from classmates, teachers, etc. One couple's strategy is to encourage their kids to do well academically so that at least they can't be 'gotten' in that area.

> Even though the kids tell him he's going to burn in hell because he believes in Nature instead of God, and that his mothers are faggots...in that environment he's still strong, because they still have to come to him for the answers, because they don't know and he does.   Anne

Even parents whose kids are young and who haven't yet

encountered major homophobia in their dealings with institutions anticipate that things will get worse as the kids get older.

> I anticipate a lot of homophobia, a lot of isolation for them, and them having to prove themselves twice as hard as everyone else because they're not from the structured family of male and female. And even though their family unit is very healthy and a heterosexual family unit is dysfunctional, they will focus in a negative way on the lesbian or gay family.   Fay

The homophobia and heterosexism encountered by lesbian parents, particularly the powerful lack of validation of the non-biological parent, can lead to doubts on the part of lesbian parents *and* their children about the legitimacy of their families. The pressure of always having to defend your right to parent can undermine your confidence in your role.

> When we were dealing with family pressures, that's when we would notice our biological role with the kids, and it would cause us conflict because then we might get fearful that I'm seeing Karl more as my child and she's seeing Marie more as her child.   Barb

Children, too, are vulnerable to external pressures.

> Sometimes, someone will say in front of the kids, 'So you're Karl's mom and you're Marie's mom.' That's really the hardest because you have to watch them experiencing people's rather heartbreaking confusion, and maybe it sets them a little bit doubtful. 'Are..are..aren't

you my mom? What do you mean I'm yours, she's hers?' 　　Anne

New Definitions

By their simple insistence on their right to parent, as well as through the parenting roles that they are developing, lesbian parents profoundly challenge the patriarchal model which defines roles through biology. In particular, the non-biological lesbian mother defies traditional notions of parenthood in that she has neither biological connection nor legal status as a parent. She is forging new ground and her existence calls for new definitions of "family" and "parent."

Jo Van Every, in her article on British social policy and the family,[2] proposes that "family" could be defined as "an emotionally supportive network of adults and children, some of whom live together or have lived together." Brian Mossop, a Toronto gay activist who recently fought a case to get bereavement leave to attend his lover's father's funeral, argues that "family" has to be defined in terms of how members of a household *act* — sharing finances, housework, emotional support, etc. — and not in terms of legal status like "spouse."[3]

Both definitions imply that people would be defined as parents *based on the act of parenting*. These definitions also challenge the economic dependence of women and children on men and put the responsibility for the care of people in need, including children, back in the public sphere.

Thinking about the redefinitions that need to take place in order to include lesbian families as legitimate families raises other important questions, beginning with the terminology lesbians are using to describe their parenting roles. All the women I interviewed consider themselves "two mothers" and want their children to refer to them using

some form of "mommyism." Is our desire to be "two mothers" a buying into the traditional model, an example of our
consciousness being more developed than our actions? Are
we using the term "mother" because that is all we know? Is
there another term that would more usefully describe the
act of parenting children? Or, on the other hand, is our
insistence on the use of the term *mother* to describe a
non-biological lesbian parent a radical redefining of the
term and a challenge to the notion that everybody only has
one mother? Is a suggestion that we call ourselves "parents"
instead a subtle rejection of the legitimacy of the non-biological "mother"? Again, lesbians are faced with the choice
of redefining and reclaiming or redefining and renaming.

This question is linked to the debate currently being
waged in the lesbian and gay community about spousal
rights. Is a fight for state-sanctioned lesbian and gay marriage, and the rights and privileges that go along with it, an
embracing of an oppressive, patriarchal institution and a
forsaking of the rich and varied alternative relationship
structures lesbians and gays have created? Or, is a struggle
for spousal rights a way to obtain immediate gains (e.g.,
employer and state-sponsored income support programs for
spouses, immigration rights, visiting rights in hospitals and
prisons, etc.) for coupled lesbians and gays, while continuing to fight for more radical changes that would guarantee
equal income support and other benefits to everyone in
society, regardless of marital status? How do we secure
rights for lesbian parents without re-creating relationships
of economic dependence, that is, "marriage." The lesbian
non-biological parent is not a "husband." Her experience
defies socially sanctioned definitions of family and points
the way to new forms of familial relationships, and possibly,
as one woman I interviewed said, a new kind of love.

> It's a different love, but it's as big a love, or as love a love. Marie (biological child) and I are forced on each other in a physical way. Conversely, with Karl (non-biological child) there's a different deep, sort of philosophical part of the love.   Anne

More research needs to be done focusing on the experience of the non-biological lesbian parent, including the emotional aspects of her experience, as well as looking at what happens when lesbian couples break up in terms of custody and visitation rights. Lesbian couples who adopt might provide an important contrast, even though in Canada, to date, only one woman can be the legal parent.

Lesbian families offer an alternative vision to the seemingly unchanging model of the nuclear family with which we are all so familiar. We need to learn from each other's experiences as we continue in our ongoing struggles to create and define our own families.

Supporting Lesbian Families: Policy Proposals

A public policy that takes into account the needs of lesbian parents and lesbian families needs to begin with a redefinition of "family" by which the defining characteristic becomes emotional or social relationships and *not* biology. Specific policy implications based on such a redefinition should include:

- The establishment of women-centred, women-controlled, government-subsidized sperm banks, accessible to any woman requiring the service.
- Giving legal parenting status to non-biological parents, based on the act of parenting.
- Legalizing second-parent adoptions (same-sex or oth-

erwise) in cases where the biological parent is still alive and actively parenting.

- Allowing parents to assign any surname they choose to their children.
- In cases of child custody disputes, allowing the "best interests of the child" to be based on relevant criteria, such as caring environment, safety and stability, and not on racist, sexist, heterosexist or ablest notions.[4]
- The reorganization of work to account for the responsibilities of parents. This would include paid parental leave for anybody involved in the parenting of a child, followed by the possibility of part-time employment without the risk of losing seniority, promotion possibilities, etc.
- Universal, affordable and accessible child care available on a part-time or full-time basis. Affordability should not be dependent on low wage rates for child care workers.
- Re-evaluation of the housing needs of different family forms and government-sponsored renovations and building initiatives to accommodate these needs.
- Day cares and schools be required to have curriculum and materials that reflect alternative family forms, including lesbian and gay families.
- CRTC regulations that require all media sources to positively portray alternative family forms and to provide a specified percentage of lesbian content.
- Public education programs be carried out in all government and private institutions. Programs should address the viability and positive nature of a variety of family forms, and deal specifically with homophobia and heterosexism.

Endnotes

1. No exact figures on the numbers of children born to lesbians are available. A 1990 article in the American magazine *Newsweek* estimated that 5,000 to 10,000 lesbians had borne children after coming out. Canadian statistics are probably roughly the same, based proportionately on our population.

    In her 1991 paper "Self Insemination: An Overview of Canadian Practice," Mary Ann Coffey quotes Roberta Achtenberg, former directing attorney of the Lesbian Rights Project and current Assistant Secretary in the Fair Housing and Equal Opportunities office of the Clinton administration. She estimates that in 1988 between 1,000 and 3,000 children in the United States and Europe had been conceived by lesbians using donor insemination.

2. Jo Van Every, "Who is the 'family'? The assumptions of British social policy," Revised version of paper presented at the Canadian Sociology and Anthropology Association Annual Conference, Queens University, Kingston, Ontario, June 1-4, 1991.

3. Brian Mossop, "Brian Mossop Responds," *Xtra*, no. 219, March 19, 1993, 29.

4. Van Every, "Who is the 'family'?"

Thank you to the women who generously agreed to be interviewed for this project.

Excerpt from
The Me in the Mirror

Connie

Panzarino

I was invited to speak at the National Lesbian and Gay Pride March on Washington. As I faced the murmuring crowd of three hundred thousand people gathered at the morning rally, I thought of how far we had come, and how much farther we had to go. There was a ramp for me to get up onto the stage, but it was in the back of the stage, and poorly designed it was so steep that it took four people to help me up.

"Hi! It's good to be here. How about you, are you glad to be here?" A shout came up from the crowd. Their energy was enormous and took me by surprise. "I'm proud to be here. Proud that I'm a lesbian, proud that I'm disabled, and proud to like my body. I want to talk to you about ableism. Do you know what ableism is? Ableism is the disease that causes us to hate what's different. It's what homophobia and sexism and racism are about. Ableism says that those who are more 'able' should have more rights, more power, and more money than those who are less able." The crowd became silent. "We have all grown up in this country with this view. Ableism supports the patriarchal system which says that AIDS research must take second priority to national defense, just like all other disease research. This country hates people with any illness or disabling conditions, not just people with AIDS. We need to turn that around. We need cures and preventions for people with AIDS and all people with illnesses and disabilities. We need money for attendant care, equipment and housing for all people who need them. There's plenty of money out there." People shouted, "Yeah! Yeah!"

"We need to stop committing ableism amongst ourselves. Each time you look in the mirror and say to yourself 'I'm too fat,' or 'my skin is ugly,' or, 'I'm too skinny,'you are committing ableism. Be proud of your difference. What would a forest be like if every single tree and every leaf were identical? I have seen some very beautiful trees with twisted or broken branches.

"I'm tired of being ashamed. I'm proud of being a lesbian! And I'm proud of being disabled. It's 'nice' that they built a ramp so I could get up here to speak to you, but why are the steps in the front and the ramp in the back? Next time I want to see that ramp out front! I love you all, and I want you to love yourselves and each other."

I felt lifted up into the air by the cheering. I did not feel like a performer, or an act in a sideshow. I felt like a treasured member of a great throng, and we all agreed.

Challenging Fragmentation: White Privilege, Jewish Oppression and Lesbian Identity

Alisa Gayle-Deutsch

As I explore my experiences as a lesbian, I find myself struggling to locate them within a context of anti-lesbianism and heterosexism which is falsely separate from my experiences of other oppressions and privileges. My memories form short, disconnected vignettes, in which distinct and separate aspects of my identity are expressed. At many points I have questioned whether my focus in this piece is, in fact, related, or even valid, with regard to the theme of resisting anti-lesbianism. These moments speak to the profound ways fragmentation has impacted upon our lives and our identities. My lesbian identity is inextricably connected to my Jewishness, my white-skinned and able-bodied privilege and my western context. These thoughts reflect issues I am currently struggling with in political work and personal identity; issues largely grounded in my experiences of resisting oppression across differences with young, multiracial lesbians, Jewish women and women in university.

In our resistance to systemic silencing, invisibility and

oppression, we search for our identities through naming who we are. Yet as we attempt to define ourselves, we often internalize dominant structures of dichotomy and, thus, work within spheres of fragmentation. Fragmentation occurs along many lines. We describe "parts" of ourselves according to categories of identity without fully exploring the complexity of these identities. This alienated construct perpetuates our silence and invisibility. It prevents acknowledging the co-existence of oppression and privilege. I seek to explore the intersection of white-skin privilege *and* Jewish identity. As Elly Bulkin describes, "choosing both" actually means not just for me, but for other white-skinned Jewish women. (Bulkin, Pratt, Smith, 96) I write from my experience as a young, white, western, Ashkenazi Jewish, able-bodied, lower middle-class lesbian. I write about how fragmentation operates within a context of anti-racist work among white women and about the profound barriers which hinder our change. To begin from a framework of wholeness, I explore my own history, the complexity of my Jewish lesbian identity — including the issues of Israel/Palestine, white Jewish racism, anti-Semitism — in both a white anti-racist context and where white-skin privilege and Jewish oppression intersect.

Initially I resisted this exploration. I rationalized that it is *more* important to focus on my white-skin privilege *than* my Jewishness or my lesbian identity. These thoughts reflect the dichotomy and fragmentation I challenge. Evelyn Torton Beck raises these questions in the introduction to *Nice Jewish Girls, A Lesbian Anthology:* "Why is it often difficult to see parallels? Do we resist seeing them? Need one oppression cancel out another? Would the recognition that it is not *either/or* but *both/and* be too overwhelming?" (Beck, xxiv) A framework of inclusiveness, in which white-skin privilege and Jewish oppression co-exist, is not only a process of locating the contextual origins of our oppression, but also of resistance, through redefining my identity in its wholeness and complexity.

Split at the Root or Piecing Together

Being, as Adrienne Rich describes, "split at the root." I bring many issues, experiences and histories to my quest for wholeness. The very origin of my fragmentation is my parents' histories of both oppression and privilege. "Piecing together" my roots has been a frustrating, angering and painful process. In seeking truths, I have been met with internal and external resistance — suspicion, denial, lies and misperceptions — which, in themselves, reflect the false dichotomy of oppression vs. privilege.

Working from origins of deceit and fragmentation, I begin as one of two daughters of white university-educated, Marxist-identified American, heterosexual parents who immigrated to Canada when my father burned his draft card during the Vietnam War in 1967. My father is white, Virginian-born, Methodist-raised, the eldest son of six boys who was supposedly "active" in the African American Liberation or "Civil Rights Movement" in the South. (Given his current dedication to white supremacist ideology, anti-Semitism, lesbian and gay bashing and misogyny, it is difficult for me to accept that he once contributed positively to anti-racism and social justice.) My ancestors on my father's side arrived from England on the East Coast of the "United States" in the 1620s. From them, I inherit a history of stealing and colonizing First Nations land and enslaving African Americans. Yet, in this family legacy of racism and colonization, these well-documented histories are ironically difficult to obtain.

My mother was born in a large Ashkenazi Jewish community in Texas. She was raised in various predominantly Christian communities and spent a significant amount of her life on Long Island, New York. She grew up as a third-generation secular Jew of (to the best of our knowledge) Russian and Polish ancestry. There is confusion as to whether these relatives were all Ashkenazi or whether there were Sephardic Jews in my grandfather's family. Hours and hours poring over family trees, notes, letters, photocopies of birth certificates will never answer all the questions. Most of the documentation of my mother's family in the small, eastern European town hall records was destroyed during the Nazi Holocaust. This is not only a piece of my history which I can never find, but it is also a profound loss which haunts a deep place within me. As a result of the Holocaust, assimilation and internalized anti-Semitism, I can only know pieces. I make assumptions and continue to stare at pictures and wonder. There are parallels between the desperate struggle of my mother's family to assimilate as Jews, to deny and to disconnect from our Jewish history, and the desperate attempts of my father's family to escape the responsibility for the history of British colonization.

In trying to name my historical roots, I also recognize external resistance to this wholeness. In my own family, racism and anti-Semitism co-exist and intersect profoundly. I struggle to understand the role of inter-oppression between my parents, the many floating pieces of my history: connecting my parents' marriage and my mother's loss of her Jewish identity; how my sister and I were given two Hebrew names (Ruth and Alisa); how we were denied our Jewishness; and how despite my father's overt anti-Semitism, Holocaust denial and racism, we are both in a process of defining our Jewish identity, exploring our roots, engaged in anti-racist work and piecing together all of who we are.

"Piecing together" becomes a question of how to take responsibility for histories of both the oppressor and the oppressed. Until recently, I have neglected both histories, out of fear and resistance. I am conscious of two strong currents. White-skin privilege, which leads me to embrace my history of oppression and to deny my roots of colonization of First Nations' peoples; and internalized anti-Semitism, which leads me to assimilate and to deny my Jewish history. I feel a strong resistance to be "both" or "many." My most profound fear is that I will choose one parent's history *over* another; choose oppression *or* privilege.

I was confronted, once again, by the intersection of oppression and privilege during a visit to Dallas, Texas. My Jewish grandmother lives there, in a small, upper-class white, Ashkenazi Jewish community where white Jews' racism — specifically anti-Chicana/o and anti-Black racism — is rampant, where Jewish identity is based solely on white Ashkenazi culture and where support for Israel is as unequivocal as monthly donations to Hadassah and B'Nai Brith. How are oppression and privilege defined within this context? It is complex. It is also the embarrassment my grandmother feels when her white "half-Jewish," "darker of the two," lesbian, lower middle-class granddaughter shows up with too many questions, too much anger, too Jewish-looking and doesn't fit in at the white, Ashkenazi, upper-class synagogue.

Such realities inspire me to create and redefine my own Jewish identity, to confront white Jewish racism, to learn more about my histories and to work for a context of resistance in which I will be whole as an anti-racist, white Ashkenazi, western Jewish lesbian. To explore how our diversity transforms our experiences, I wrote an article "reviewing" the "Being Jewish and Queer" Forum at University of Toronto during Lesbian, Gay and Bisexual Awareness Week:

> Surviving in a white, male, Christian, middle-class, able-bodied, heterosexual dominated society, we are taught to view our experience of marginalization in fragmented ways. That is, we learn to be "only Jewish" in Jewish spaces and "only gay/lesbian or bisexual" in queer spaces. At the same time that we struggle to be visible and heard we also silence and hide certain "parts" of ourselves. Being exposed to anti-Semitic stereotypes which tell us that all Jews are white, upper-class and heterosexual, or that all queers are white, middle-class and Christian create a sense of fragmentation and disconnection in our lives. If we only examine our language we use to describe our communities, we can recognize that we use words which make assumptions about who we are as Jews, gays, lesbians and bisexuals. For example, we often refer to *the* Jewish Community or *the* Lesbian and Gay Community and in doing so fragment and silence.

Ironically, my critique of fragmentation and homogenization fails to fully explore the diversity of Jewish identity, the full complexity of how our experiences of oppression are *transformed* by our race, gender, sexuality, language, ethnicity, global position, ability, age and class. Challenging fragmentation of Jewish identity must be done, not only in the dominant white supremacist, Christian-culture, but also in our own Jewish communities. As white, Ashkenazi Jews we must challenge what Sephardic Jewish feminist Rita Arditti names as our total "oblivious[ness] to the existence of the Sephardim," the omission of Sephardic communities destroyed in the Holocaust or of the "Sephardim survivors of the Holocaust." I must educate myself about the histories of Sephardic Jews, Mizrachi Jews and Jews of Colour, and make the links to my position and to current oppression of these communities in western and global contexts. Resistance to challenging our racism, ableism, anti-lesbianism, imperialism and classism within Jewish communities perpetuates our fragmentation and our alienation as Jews.

I am both white *and* Jewish. When I speak with white women who discount my privilege with "but you're Jewish," I am forced to respond with "Yes, I am both Jewish and white. I both take up space and am silenced. I am both. I am more than both. I am many." However, "coming out" as Jew has been a process of resisting others' definitions of fragmentation. I am variously, "Half-Jewish, part-Jewish, completely Jewish (because my mother is Jewish), not Jewish because I am secular, not Jewish-looking enough, not Jewish because I am a lesbian, because I am lower middle class, because I am anti-Israel, because I am anti-racist, because I believe in Palestinian freedom."

This internal struggle of dichotomous identities has been reinforced by my concern about my role as an anti-racist white-skinned Jewish woman. Anti-Semitism and racism, and consequently, white Jewish women and women of Colour, are often pitted against one another. I feel that this has resulted in my own fears of naming anti-Semitism and an internalization of the anti-Semitic stereotype that, as a Jew, this will jeopardize work challenging white-skinned privilege. Unfortunately, during the process of writing this piece, my fears are consistently validated. In the political groups with which I currently work (predominantly lesbian and women's groups), anti-Semitism continues to be excluded from anti-oppression work. Simultaneously, Jews are increasingly scapegoated as the "most racist" both for white-skinned privilege and our responsibility for Israel's actions. I am haunted by a familiar phrase: "It's one thing to be white...but you're *Jewish*."

Coalition Work as a Young Lesbian

Fearing my lack of commitment to anti-racism, I denied my Jewishness and avoided "coming out" as a Jew. Similarly, I was actively in solidarity with lesbians and gays resisting anti-lesbianism, but denied my own lesbian identity. This also stemmed from my fear of "abusing" identity politics in an attempt to deny, "cancel" or "lose" my white-skin privilege through "finding a new oppression." Working as a member of Les-Bi Youth Peer Support, previously Lesbian Youth Peer Support (LYPS), I have been struck by the pervasiveness of this oppressed — therefore-unable-to-oppress mentality. It seems that we, as white women, believe that in coming out as lesbians or bisexuals we trade-in or lose our white privilege. Thus, the political bonds which we build on our "lesbian oppression" are structured by our unnamed, unmarked whiteness. Until I discussed my process of "coming out " as a Jew, I didn't recognize this.

(Documenting this aspect of my experience as a young white Jewish lesbian in LYPS has been challenging. Certainly it reflects my specific location in the group as well as my continued involvement and perceptions. Undoubtedly many other current and former women in LYPS would share very different experiences and interpretations of LYPS' herstory.)

By coming together and coming out as young multi-racial lesbians and bisexual women at LYPS we express our

resistance to anti-lesbianism and heterosexism in our families, communities, schools, workplaces, streets, "feminist"
community. However, uniting in coalition work as multi-racial lesbian and bisexual youth, we, as white women, have
imposed not only this dichotomy of oppression, but also our
racism and white dominance. We failed to validate women
of Colour's experiences, we denied our racism and assumed
we could continue working together against one oppression
without challenging our privileges and abilities to oppress.
As white, middle-class women in LYPS, we imposed a universal definition of young lesbian experience. In doing so,
we effectively invalidated many young lesbian and bisexual
women's struggles of survival and resistance. However,
despite our resistance to this work, as white-skinned
women, I believe that LYPS is at an amazing point of trans-
formation.

My perception and understanding of LYPS' history as a
lesbian and bisexual youth group is largely formed by stories and pieces from various current and former group
members; however, it has also been a process of locating
myself as a white Jewish lesbian and taking responsibility
for my own contribution to white women's racism in LYPS.
My perception of LYPS at my first meeting (approximately
two years after the group was founded) was of the "painful
struggle of young marginalized women with few resources
resisting homophobia."[1] Certainly, this is a reality; however,
this is only *one* of the many aspects of resistance for a
coalition of multi-racial lesbian and bisexual youth.

Although when I initially came to LYPS, women of Colour continued to play important leadership roles, white
women clearly dominated and created the definitions of
lesbian and bisexual existence. For example, white facilita-
tors defined external problems at LYPS as family, school

(usually university) and society, homophobia and ageism, while internal problems were subtly blamed upon women of Colour. Racism, anti-Semitism and white-skinned privilege were usually given token mentions or intellectualized in discussions facilitated by white women. That many of the divisions occurring in LYPS were between white women and women of Colour was conveniently left out in the retelling of events. A more accurate description of LYPS at that time would have been that the founders and organizers were women of Colour and that, in fact, LYPS was once a safe space for women of Colour. A true history would have located white women's failure to unlearn and challenge racism, white privilege and power, as responsible for white women's hijacking of LYPS from women of Colour. Women of Colour were leaving the group in large numbers and white women were continuing to avoid actually *doing* anti-racist work by spending endless meetings discussing *how* to organize anti-racist workshops. Finally, several white women committed to action and organized two workshops facilitated by a white Jewish woman who had been involved in the Women's Press anti-racist struggle. From that point, there began to be an acknowledgement and naming of the real issues at LYPS and, finally, the white women began to discuss our responsibility for racism at LYPS.

One of the first steps was to deconstruct our myth that simply because we are lesbian and bisexual youth, we are powerless and persecuted and, consequently, without privilege and the ability to oppress. It has meant recognizing the power and privilege located in the mainstream "Lesbian Community" phrase "but we're all the same because we're lesbians." It has also meant recognizing that resistance to anti-lesbianism must be inclusive of resistance to all forms of oppression is an organizing principle that continues to be essential in challenging this framework of fragmentation and committing to anti-racist work

Since then, LYPS has continued to struggle with actualizing our anti-racist politics. Our commitment to revitalizing a coalition of multi-racial lesbian, bisexual and Two-Spirited youth has meant developing practical policies and guidelines for anti-racism. Mandatory anti-racist workshops for *all* white women in LYPS, solidarity work with lesbian and bisexual women of Colour and Two-Spirited women of the First Nations, and integration of anti-racism in all aspects of the group have now become concrete commitments. Our process continues to be struggling as lesbian and bisexual youth to create a coalition, where white women are anti-racist, are relinquishing white-skinned privilege and power and where we work within an inclusive and *whole* context of our experiences. Despite the lack of models for this work, I believe that we strive to work critically and to openly and honestly share our struggles and process, with as many women as possible, so that we can learn from each other, challenge each other and commit to being a coalition of resistance on all levels.

White-skinned *and* Jewish

One of the most important aspects of this work is challenging the construct of fragmentation. The false dichotomization of oppression and privilege seems to work as a math equation in which one cancels out the other. This construction is a powerful root of our fragmentation. Within such a disconnected framework, "piecing together" my identity and history would result in denying my privilege or, conversely, consciousness of my white-skin privilege would result in denying my Jewishness and experience of anti-Semitism. The destructive conclusion of this mentality is that white Jewish women cannot be visibly and actively Jewish and anti-racist.

In the LYPS' white women anti-racist working group the issue of defining "white" arose. I was emphatic that we focus on white-skin privilege at our workshops. "We are not addressing many forms of oppression such as classism, ableism, ageism *and anti-Semitism* but that does not mean they are not deeply interconnected and do not need to be challenged. It also does not mean that anti-Semitism is not a form of racism." I believe all of this strongly; yet I was confused by feelings of defensiveness, disconnection and pain when I spoke these words. I realized that my anger and frustration stemmed from white non-Jewish women's reactions: "But you're Jewish" was offered to absolve me of my white skin privilege.

Why is it that resisting or naming oppression means denying or avoiding white privilege? I face a paradoxical struggle arguing — as the only Jewish woman there — that I have white skin, and that is why we're here. I felt my authenticity as a Jew being questioned. My process of "piecing together" was used to question the validity of my experience. I sat there in anger at myself for feeling distracted by this bizarre contradiction. It was clear to me there was no room in this anti-racist workshop to be white-skinned and Jewish. Not only could I not be *both,* but I cannot be *whole* in their minds.

In an attempt to not be the anti-Semitic stereotype of the "loud," "pushy," "victimized," "oppressed," "persecuted" Jew I sat there in silence, wondering how to be a white Jewish woman engaged in anti-racist work with white non-Jewish women. It is so painful. But anti-racist, anti-oppression and coalition work is essential and, therefore, must mean a commitment to working from places of commonality and difference. I experience frustration and anger when we choose to not fully explore our identities, and commit to challenging all our places of privilege. This means white non-Jewish anti-racist activists naming their anti-Semitism, educating themselves — beyond "placing it on the agenda" — and making a commitment to challenge their anti-Jewish racism.

How do we expect to fight oppression when we complacently work within a structure of dichotomy, silence and denial? How can we work together as white-skinned women and not force Jewish women to be homogenous, to "pass" in, what Melanie Kaye/Kantrowitz describes as "culture erasure, assimilation, self-hate" (Kaye/Kantrowitz, 99), silence or invisibility. We can only come together in coalition when there is commitment to include working on anti-Jewish racism. We must also be vigilant in our coalition work with women of Colour and First Nations women. Barbara Smith, in her contribution to *Yours in Struggle* challenged Black women's anti-Semitism and simultaneously challenged the characterization of "Black and/or women of colour as being more anti-Semitic and much less concerned about combating anti-Semitism than white non-Jewish women." (Bulkin, Pratt, Smith, 74) These polarizations create divisions between marginalized women. We must locate the origins of our oppression within a white, Christian-dominated heterosexist society.

A Jewish Lesbian in Academia

My experience in a first-year women's studies course at the University of Toronto reflected a larger context of both subtly encouraged and logically inevitable fragmentation. Despite the inclusive analysis initially presented in the introductory women's studies course, it primarily operated within a model of fragmentation. Not only were racism, classism, ableism and anti-lesbianism not integrated into the analysis of gender oppression, but each form of oppression was described as mutually exclusive.

I was frustrated, and angry, but silent many times throughout this course when our class lecture was given by a white woman who failed to locate herself carefully, censoring out language of massacre, genocide and her own location; when racism was virtually a footnote at the end of the lecture; when women of Colour, First Nations and mixed-race women were omitted and tokenized; when our historical discussion omitted the Holocaust; when our discussion of colonialism omitted Israel/Palestine; when our race analysis omits anti-Semitism; when the lecture devoted to women's cultural production and the historical silencing of women silences women of Colour, First Nations women and Jewish women. Frustrated and angry, but silent. My failure to speak of omission, oppression, privilege and silence throughout the course reflects my privileges and my acceptance of the fragmentation paradigm.

Interpretation of the silence and omission of Jews as solely anti-Semitism is grounded in anti-Jewish stereotypes: all Jews are white, straight, Ashkenazi, able-bodied, upper-class members of an homogenous group. In that course, the white professor failed to name those who died in the Triangle Shirt Fire in New York as mostly working-class, Ashkenazi Jewish women. This recognition and visibility would have challenged anti-Semitic stereotypes; however, anti-Semitism had not been named as a form of oppression. Omissions which fail to recognize the complexity of Jewish identity are based on stereotypes of Jewish women as pushy, loud, persecuted, Jewish American Princesses, upper-class, white, Ashkenazi, Hebrew school, pro-Israel and Zionist.

Jewish women are conveniently not visible in anti-racist work. I find myself in a framework of fragmentation, invisibility and silence. I am unable to both "take up space" as a white-skinned woman with middle-class, able-bodied privilege *and* to be silenced as a Jew and a lesbian. I am silent in the face of anti-Semitism, torn by the dichotomy of white-skin privilege and Jewishness. I leave my Jewishness at the door. I assimilate and "pass."

Israel/Palestine

Another fragmentation of my whole, white, Jewish, lesbian identity has been the question of Israel/Palestine. These issues are not only always close to me on an emotional and political level, but they have been central to my resistance to my Jewishness. Once again, false dichotomous equations constructed by white Christians have worked as barriers to defining my identity. As Ashkenazi, lesbian feminist activist Irena Klepfisz writes: "It's even harder to ignore inaccurate and anti-Semitic equations: Israeli=Jew=Israel=all Jews, and Israel government policies=Nazi policies during the Holocaust." These equations have silenced me as a Jew and as an anti-imperialist activist. These equations terrify me into believing that speaking out on Israel/Palestine will mean silencing Jewish experiences of the Holocaust and anti-Semitism.

Acting in wholeness means situating Israel/Palestine in an anti-racist framework. We cannot dismiss our location in this discussion. The Israeli government's racism not only impacts upon Arabs and Palestinians, but also on Sephardic Jews, Arab Jews, Jews of Colour, lesbians and women. There are many complex issues to discuss; however, in a climate of anti-Semitism and racism they are often resisted and avoided. They are considered too painful. I ask, too painful for whom? As a white, western Jewish woman standing on First Nations land, who am I silencing when I fail to name Israel's racism, colonization? Why is it that we avoid the links?

Despite this intellectual analysis and framework, as I write this I am struggling with a sudden resistance to being Jewish. With the news that "A Jewish settler has murdered…" I feel desperate to deny my Jewishness in relation to Israel. I write the following poem:

yet the screams are muffled
by our Western media
thoughts of media-control, so-called Jewish conspiracy
overpower my thoughts
when colonial power is unquestioned
when racism is sanctioned
and I — a lesbian — would not be

thoughts on a rainy morning
preparing my topic for women's studies — safe,
I discuss
anti-Semitism

I desperately try to divorce myself
Anglicize myself
as I read
"Jewish settler…"

as Zionism speaks for me

Despite my belief that Zionism has operated as a mask for racism, anti-Semitism and colonialism, and despite my belief that my only connection to Israel is what is done in my name as a Jew, I am hard-pressed to remember a time of such personal confusion and turmoil. My mother faced a similar dilemma. In New York, in her early twenties — and after marrying my extremely anti-Semitic father — my mother became enraged with what she perceived as unconditional, unquestioned and unequivocal support for Israel during the 1967 June War. In her strength and courage to name colonialism, racism and injustice, she, too, equated her Jewishness with Israel and consciously decided she could not be *both*. This is perhaps one of the most painful aspects of my "piecing together." Piecing together my own loss and that of my mother's, as we have been denied our Jewishness because of anti-Semitism, racism, assimilation, Zionism. We have not been allowed to be all of who we are.

Coming Together

In the time since I began to write this piece, I have been given the gift of finding two unique and wonderful spaces of wholeness. The first is in the abyss of university where, originally, nine white Jewish women and I have begun to create a framework of wholeness. We have created a political discussion group in which we are white and Jewish, Sephardic and Ashkenazi, lesbian and straight, working-class and middle-class, and a variety of ages. It is a space where we discuss our racism and our internalized anti-Semitism. Where we discuss that we are the elite of Jews — the privileged — that yes, in fact, we are white Jews and Jews of Colour are not here in this space with us, but do exist. It is also a space where we discuss the issue of Israel/Palestine and I am able to express my belief that we must stand in solidarity with Palestinian women fighting the oppression of Israel.

The second unique space is the Jewish Women's Committee to End the Occupation of the West Bank and Gaza. Although I am relatively new in this group and to work as a Jewish woman against Israel's occupation of Palestine, I am immeasurably grateful and overwhelmed by its very existence. Having found this space, where I am able to work politically with all of who I am as a young Jewish Lesbian against the Occupation, moves me very deeply. It also makes me painfully aware of my fragmentation in LYPS and many other spaces and has inspired me to redefine resistance.

The paradigm of fragmentation not only denies our experiences, it also operates as a barrier to our political work. Fragmentation compounds our divisions and places obstacles between us. Our alienation can be challenged. We can create new contexts for wholeness and for being actively and visibly Jewish and white. I am inspired by women in my life who have created a context for the beginning of my process and who demand wholeness from me in every aspect of my life. I am inspired and challenged by lesbians, bisexual and straight women of Colour, by First Nations and Two-Spirited women who are generous in their patience, knowledge and sharing of experience in coalition work with white Jewish women. I am inspired by non-Jewish lesbians who have worked with me in anti-racist workshops and gone home to work on their anti-Semitism, who have called me Jewish when I could not; by the many diverse Jewish women in my family and in our communities, who have written, spoken, shared their visions for change, for connectedness and wholeness; by the women who have spoken out in solidarity with Palestinian women when I thought my mother and I were the only ones; by women challenging the painful response of fragmentation in the face of oppression; by women who challenge oppression in all its forms every day, and still have time to write the courage to be all of who they are.

Endnote

1. I have attempted to avoid using the terms "homophobia" and "lesbophobia" in my own definitions of resistance. Despite their prevalence in our vocabulary describing our experiences as lesbian and bisexual women as a psychiatric survivor, I believe that it is essential that we locate these terms as psychiatric language of pathologizing and labeling which must be challenged.

Sources

Beck, Evelyn Torton, ed. *Nice Jewish Girls — A Lesbian Anthology.* Boston, MA: Beacon Press, 1989.

Bendt, Ingela. *We Shall Return — Women in Palestine.* London, England: Zed Press Ltd., 1980.

Bulkin, Elly, Minnie Bruce Pratt, and Barbara Smith. *Yours in Struggle: Three Feminist Perspectives on Anti-Semitism and Racism.* Ithaca, New York: Firebrand Books, 1988.

Fireweed. no. 35 (spring 1992).

Frankenburg, Ruth. *White Women, Race Matters: The Social Construction of Whiteness.* Minneapolis: University of Minnesota Press, 1993.

"From the Mouth to the Page," *Fireweed* 40, no. 39 (summer 1993).

Jewish Women's Committee to End the Occupation of the West Bank and Gaza. *Jewish Women's Call For Peace: A Handbook for Jewish Women on the Israeli/Palestinian Conflict.* Ithaca, New York: Firebrand Books, 1990.

Kaye/Kantrowitz, Melanie. *The Issue is Power — Essays on Women, Jews, Violence and Resistance.* San Francisco, CA: aunt lute books, 1992.

Klepfisz, Irena. *Dreams of an Insomniac: Jewish Feminist Essays, Speeches and Diatribes.* Portland, Oregon: Eighth Mountain Press, 1990.

McIntosh, Peggy, "White Privilege: Unpacking the Invisible Knapsack," *Peace and Freedom* (July/August, 1989).

Siegal, Rachel Josefowitz. *Jewish Women in Therapy: Seen But Not Heard.* London, England: 1990.

Wearing Our Identity

Deborah L. Repplier

As a lesbian, I must continually come out, defining my sexual orientation against predominant heterosexist beliefs. Sometimes this means responding directly to naive questions about whether I'm married or dating any interesting men. Other times this means actively seeking the opportunity to speak up, to let someone know that the person s/he has befriended, respected, admired, etc., is in fact a lesbian. Every situation is different. Choosing to tell someone I am a lesbian is as much a statement about me and my self-perception as about how I regard the individual involved. To not tell someone is a pretty big comment about perceived narrow-mindedness and bigotry, just as to come forward in an instance of intimacy addresses a sense of perceived trust and awareness. As I meet new people in the many contexts of day-to-day life, I continually make the decision about whether or not to disclose my identity, whether or not to come out. And this means disclosing not just the gender of whom I have sex with, but also whom I live with, whom I make a home with, travel with — whom I love and who I am. Coming out is not always an easy decision to make. Each situation must be assessed for both physical and emotional safety. I know this. And I expect this. What I did not expect, however, is that even after I come out to individuals who seemingly respect my identity, respect is not always there — as I recently discovered spending the holidays with my partner's family.

Telling this story fills me with a great sense of disillusionment, anger, and yes, pain, for when you are constantly invalidated, mistreated and monsterized by the world at large, you expect more from those individuals who profess understanding, acceptance and respect. My partner came out to her parents at the age of eighteen — twelve years ago. Having a mother who calls herself "feminist," and a gay older brother who had already defined himself as such, the path was somewhat trodden for her. Since that time, twelve years ago, she has had intimate relationships only with women. Her brother was in a long-term relationship of thirteen and a half years with a man before dying of AIDS. Combine this with the fact that she and I have committed ourselves to one another for life, albeit without benefit of public or legal ceremony, and the message is pretty clear: we are gay. So it was with great surprise that I first heard the conversation between my partner and her parents, as my partner conveyed to me.

The issue of coming out came up in discussion. Both her parents were adamant about lesbians and gays remaining closeted. Said her father: "People who are secure with themselves have no need to discuss their sexuality." (Read: telling people you are lesbian or gay means you are insecure.) Said her mother: "Why do you need to label yourself? If people ask about your private life, tell them *you just haven't met the right man yet*." (Emphasis mine!) Let me qualify here that the mother speaks from her experience of knowing three "radical lesbian feminists" who, during the 1970s, wanted nothing to do with men, and who are now married to men — or two of them anyway. These women, in the mother's mind, proved their identity was not fixed, thus creating the possibility that her daughter's identity as a lesbian could change, as well. The mother then went on to say that you should not tell others about your sexual orientation because (1) in most places it is illegal to be homosexual, and (2) people shouldn't use labels anyway. Of course, this latter comment followed our dinner party of the previous evening, in which the mother introduced all around the table according to social and marital relation: "my daughter-in-law," "my mother," "my daughter," all except me, introduced only as "Deborah." But let us remember to always adhere to a label-free world.

Now, it seems clear to me that what both parents fail to recognize is that being lesbian or gay means much more than simply fucking women or men, respectively. And that accepting who you are means having the pride to not conceal your identity — or your partner's identity — out of shame or fear, despite the countering messages sent to us from every direction of society. What they refuse to understand is that being a lesbian speaks to more than sexuality, but also to who we love. Whom we trust. Whom we laugh with. Whom we talk to and share with, everything from our innermost beliefs to the mundane happenings of our daily lives. It's not just about whom we sleep with, but whom we wake up to. Whom we choose to build our lives with, and how we choose to live those lives. It's about taking risks sometimes, just to hold hands outside of the sanctity of home. It's about knowing that you exist, and your partner exists, and your friends exist, and that you are normal, productive, responsible contributors to society, even though you are virtually invisible in the media, or worse, imaged as child-molesting, man-hating, family-bashing perverts. In Hollywood, lesbians pretty much corner the market on psychotic female killers, with gay men holding their own, as well.

When I come forward and tell someone that I am lesbian, I am referring to a way of life that is political, social, economical and sexual. To fail to recognize this complexity reduces who we are as lesbians and gay men to a sexual act — a devaluation that happens all too frequently. When I first came out to my family, one sister's candid response was, "I felt OK about your being gay, *until I started imagining what you do in bed*." (Again, my emphasis!) Well, had I not been so quick to embrace any acceptance on her part, my response *should* have been that I felt OK with her heterosexuality, until I began thinking about what she and her husband do in bed, but I'm afraid the absurdity would have been lost.

Though my sister's response is insulting, it is not an isolated one. This same mentality is being voiced right now by opponents of the bill that would lift the ban on gays in the United States military. There is so much talk about the morale of the soldiers who would feel *uncomfortable* with the thought of showering with or sleeping near someone who is gay — (Read: men who might want to fuck me and women who definitely don't.) — as if gay people are indiscriminate in their sexual activity. Many of these same people have suggested that gays should be allowed to serve their country as long as they remain closeted, relying on the old what-you-do-in-your-bedroom-is-your-business argument. But this, too, reduces us to being only the perpetrators of sexual acts.

Continual denial of our personhood, forced invisibility in the culture at large, and media focus on disparaging stereotypes, all contribute not just to the detriment of the gay community, but to the detriment of society as a whole. When social discrimination and intolerance against any group is a common legal practice, as is certainly the case in the U.S. military as well as in the state of Colorado these days, this can be construed as a free licence to bash. It comes as no surprise that the passage of Amendment 2[1] in Colorado has witnessed a marked increase in violence against gays in that state. And when violence is pervasive in any aspect of society, it is detrimental to all, and most particularly to those who are the target. When gays are bashed daily on the streets, when this violation of our basic human rights is sanctioned by the government's refusal to perceive it as a crime of hate, then the message about our social worth does not leave much room for ambiguity.

When we are backed into a closet, let out only with whips and chains — or ice-picks, as Hollywood would have it — when we respond to heterosexist assumptions about our sexuality with the comment that we "just haven't met the right man yet," then we internalize the shame that is showered upon us and condone, albeit silently, the discrimination and violence hurled against us as lesbians, bisexuals and gay men. When we speak out and speak up, when we come out of the closet and wear our identity on our sleeves or pink triangles on our lapels, when we label ourselves as gays, or lesbians, or bisexuals, then we are anything but insecure with our sexuality. We are proud and accepting of who we are politically, socially and sexually. We are demanding the respect that is rightfully ours by speaking out against intolerance and discrimination.

Endnote

1. Amendment 2, which appeared on the Colorado State ballet in November 1992, repealed existing local anti-discrimination protection for lesbians and gays, in housing, employment and public accommodations in Denver, Boulder and Aspen. It prohibited any municipality, county or state anti-discrimination

protections from ever being enacted. Since the writing of this article, I am pleased to convey, Amendment 2 was stricken down by the highest Colorado State Court and as of late December 1993 it is no longer in effect.

The Cultivation of Queerness: Parenting My Way into the 21st Century

Elise Chenier

After thirty-six hours of increasingly intense labour, I could barely lift my head off the delivery table. The epidural had worked its magic, letting me sleep between contractions during the final few hours. But I wasn't about to miss watching this baby squeeze itself out. After all, I spent the previous month not really believing it was possible.

With his hands slipped under the baby's armpits, my ob/gyn gently lifted it from between my legs. I strained to catch sight of this rather gruesome but somehow natural act. With the baby's belly now fully visible to me, I quietly lay my head back down on the styrofoam pillow.

"It's a boy," I said.

"No...wait," my sister-cum-coach insisted, "that's the umbilical cord."

No longer needing a push, the feet slid out easily. My doctor hurriedly began suctioning out the baby's nose and throat before handing it over to me. My sister grabbed me by my shoulders.

"It's a girl," she screamed.

I never made any bones about the fact that I wanted a girl. Only amongst the most suburban of my friends and acquaintances did this cause any kind of discomfort. Otherwise, it was deemed a reasonable longing for a young woman who was most likely going to be raising a child alone. However, my declaration that I hope my daughter is a lesbian continues to ruffle more than a few feathers.

Predictably, gay-friendly straights think that I am unfairly imposing my own values upon my daughter and are concerned that my biased ideals will ultimately restrict her natural development. Uh-huh. Of course, the fact that I just as passionately hope she, like myself, loves books, goes to university and brushes her teeth every day receives nods of approval all around. But then again, literacy, education and personal hygiene are not values, are they? It's only right to want what's best for one's children. Truth is, we know what the song and dance is about.

The indictment is so predictable that it's boring. The reaction I get from "my own kind" is far more interesting. While I think that, at least part of the now-familiar reproachful glance is inspired by the exact same kind of thinking typical of our "concerned" gay-positive friends and neighbours, there is another, more insidious discomfort, that makes some people not only squirm but also want to distance themselves from such an irresponsible dyke. To wilfully encourage a child to be a homosexual threatens to crack one of the *central* pillars upon which the gay rights movement has attempted to make inroads in our homophobic culture. Homosexuals, we repeatedly declare, do not recruit. Frankly, I suspect my life would have been a lot simpler if there *had* been an information booth at my Catholic school Fun Fair. Nevertheless, I refuse to mollycoddle the homophobic fear of a massive social sexual disorientation. It's just not going to happen. Thank God.

So, if we know it's not going to happen, why compromise ourselves to those who live in fear of it? For me, it's not just about queer politics. It's also about parenting. And it's not just about parenting, either. It's also about being a mother. Not one to balk tradition, I take my responsibility as purveyor of culture seriously. But whose culture? Which culture?

To us urban queers, being gay is something that goes far beyond our controversial choice of love/sex object. Our sexual practice impacts on the clubs we go to, the books we read, the movies we see and the ridiculous T-shirts we wear. It influences the charities to which we donate, the political leaders for whom we vote and, sometimes, the schools to which we send our children. In my daughter's world, women can marry women, men can wear dresses and sex is like a massage between two special people who may or may not live together or be married.

No one owns my daughter's sexuality, least of all me. But she will never have to hide out in some trailer park on the outskirts of town, afraid and uncertain of who she is and what the afterlife will bring to bear on her kind. When she walks into a college pub for the first time, she will know that this is not all there is; that, straight, gay or bi, there is always more than one way of being. This, I think, is one of the best things I can offer her. And if that's recruiting, then call me Officer.

Liberté, Égalité, Sororité

Candis Graham

Let us never cease from thinking, — what is this
"civilization" in which we find ourselves? What are
these ceremonies and why should we take part in them?
What are these professions and why should we make
money out of them? Where in short is it leading us, the
procession of the sons of educated men?

Virginia Woolf

I want to change the world. I believe we change the world
by changing ourselves and sharing ourselves with others.
This is what I am trying to do. I constantly question my
attitudes and motives and feelings, and continually challenge my fears so I can change. Day after day I am learning
to live my life with integrity.

From books and from friends I learn to be what I call
political. This is where I get most of my ideas, my strength,
my faith and my beliefs. Women friends and books written
by women nourish my dreams, stimulate my mind, feed my
soul, guide my spirit and teach me to listen to my body.

Friends

In the summer of 1974, I met two women who started a revolution in my life.

Marie Robertson, a lesbian activist, taught me to take pride in being a lesbian. She rejoices in her lesbian self and is out in all aspects of her life.

Marie showed me a hidden and clandestine world. I discovered lesbians are everywhere, although I had not noticed even one before. She took me to the Blue Jay, a lesbian nightclub in Toronto. How can I describe the joy I felt that first time, sitting in a huge room filled with women? I was so enchanted that for days I told everyone I met, including straight women and men, that there was nothing to compare with watching women dance with women.

In December 1974 Marie and I and three other women decided to rent a house together. We found a house which seemed suitable but when we talked to the landlord, he said, "You're lesbians, aren't you?" Marie said, "Yes." He said he would have to increase the rent because "you have to pay for being lesbians."

We were astonished and indignant and angry. We went to the Human Rights Commission to lodge a complaint and learned this man could legally discriminate against lesbians. Marie talked to a gay activist in Toronto about possible options and we decided to take the issue to the media. We met with an apparently sympathetic journalist. He wrote an article for the Kitchener-Waterloo newspaper that included our names, ages and addresses.

For weeks I lived with acute fear, wondering if queer bashers would appear at my door. I was afraid to be alone. I was afraid to answer the door or the phone. There were a few supportive calls from people, and some obscene callers, too. I was more out than I had ever been and I had never felt such fear.

The story was picked up by other newspapers, including *The Body Politic* and other mainstream papers in Toronto and Ottawa. I finally understood that the discrimination was newsworthy because we were lesbians and that is considered sensational. My life was lurid, and the circumstances didn't really matter.

The next time we went to a gay dance on the outskirts of Waterloo, we saw the landlord standing near the door to the men's washroom. Marie made a few enquiries and learned he was in the habit of selling his body to other men in public washrooms.

I met Margaret Telegdi at the University of Waterloo's Birth Control Centre, where we were volunteers. Margaret, a radical feminist, introduced me to the politics of the women's liberation movement and inspired me to take pride in being a woman. She took me to the self-health group she had started with another woman at Women's Place in Waterloo. I inserted a plastic speculum in my vagina and nervously peered inside, with help from a flashlight and a mirror. The other women stood as far away as they could get in that small room. One by one they came forward. Soon women were crowded around me, wanting to see my cervix. Soon each woman was excited and impatient to look at her self.

This was an exciting new concept to me, women learning about our own bodies and taking responsibility for our health. A few months earlier I had left nursing for, among other reasons, my feeling that the health care system was oppressive, devoid of dignity and compassion for anyone who needed health care.

I read everything I could about the women's liberation

movement. Page after page, I knew this time we were going to go further than women had ever dreamed of. We were going to completely change the world.

In 1975 I moved to Ottawa, which had larger communities of feminist activists and gay activists.

With Margaret's encouragement and thanks to her enthusiasm, in 1976 I organized two weekend courses of Wen-Do self-defense for women. Margaret came to Ottawa to teach us. I can still see women breaking boards and taboos with their bare hands, still hear their shouts. I felt we were uncovering our power.

Around the same time, Marie and I went to a gay conference at Queen's University in Kingston. Lesbian autonomy became an issue because some of the gay men didn't understand and resented our determination to meet without them. We were surprised and disappointed, but we had our own workshops.

As a result of that experience, Marie agreed to organize a national lesbian conference. I worked with her and a small group of dykes. We called ourselves LOON (Lesbians of Ottawa Now). The conference was held at the University of Ottawa in October 1976. I walked around the campus grinning from ear to ear as I passed smiling lesbians. As well as being a wild success and great fun, the conference was inspirational. Afterwards, political and social groups of lesbians were formed in various parts of Canada.

I want to live with caring and compassion for myself and others, but there's a lot I still haven't figured out. I don't know what to do about friends who hurt other women (not just in intimate relationships but in other relationships such as employee-employer) and my inclination to reject them completely for their abusive behaviour.

Friends are my source of lesbian energy. They show me

the ways of insurrection. Through the years I have been blessed with some precious friendships and I try to be a good friend to the women I know — to be open, to listen, respond, share, believe, trust, accept — and to like and love each one.

I think loving friendships are one way we change the world.

Books

In 1974 I went to the Toronto Women's Bookstore and found my first books about lesbians: *The Well of Loneliness* (Radclyffe Hall), *Rubyfruit Jungle* (Rita Mae Brown), *The Cook and The Carpenter* (June Arnold), *Riverfinger Women* (Elana Nachman, now Elana Dykewomon), *Lesbian Woman* (Del Martin and Phyllis Lyon) and *Patience and Sarah* (Isabel Miller). I read each one over and over, except *The Well of Loneliness* which I read only once.

In 1975, after attending an inspirational lesbian conference in Montreal, Marie and I decided to establish a library of lesbian books at the Waterloo Women's Place. The gay liberation group at the University of Waterloo gave Marie about $200 (which seemed like a small fortune) and one of our friends, Kate, went to the Toronto Women's Bookstore and came back with armfuls of books. Then we were told that the collective of mostly non-lesbians who managed the house were upset. They didn't believe a lesbian library was necessary. They wanted us to remove or combine the lesbian books with the house library. We were indignant and disappointed. Why weren't they pleased to have a lesbian library at Women's Place?

This was my first experience, but not my last, with the lesbophobia of straight feminists and closeted lesbians.

In addition to books, through the 1980s and into the

1990s I have been influenced, guided, encouraged and in-spired by two incredible journals: *Common Lives/Lesbian Lives* and *Sinister Wisdom.* These publications present me with ideas and perspectives that I don't always get from my friends. I have been challenged by the issues of *Sinister Wisdom* on passing, disability, class, surviving psychiatric assault and creating emotional well-being in our communi-ties, and the fiction in *Common Lives,* especially the stories on abuse and body sizes/shapes.

Writing, publishing, selling/buying, sharing and read-ing books are another way we change the world.

Politics

I love the 1970s slogan "the personal is political." To live as a lesbian is personal and extremely political. I revere the work done by lesbians within lesbian organizations, within feminist organizations, within lesbian/gay/bisexual organi-zations. I need lesbians working as lesbians wherever we chose to work for change.

I don't always come out, although I do not always have the choice. I know the dangers and fears. I have seen lesbo-phobia force some lesbians into self-destructive lives — lying, hiding, isolation, abuse by psychiatrists, alcohol and/or drug abuse, marrying men, suicide. Sometimes I "forget" to be political. There are times when my life feels like a relentless struggle to survive. I am preoccupied with acquiring and keeping decent waged work. Or I am search-ing for a pleasant, affordable place to live. Sometimes I am exhausted by my feelings of resentment, frustration and anger about the way women, and especially lesbians, are treated in this world. Sometimes I feel only my fears and anxieties. Sometimes I want to hide.

I am out almost everywhere. It is a freeing feeling.

I rejoice every time a lesbian comes out anywhere — each coming out is important and makes it easier for me to come out. Being able to come out and celebrate being a lesbian is paramount to self-esteem and self-love. This, I sense, is one of the ways we change and create a vastly different world.

Writing

Since 1977 I have worked for part-time wages so I can devote time and energy to writing. I believe writing as a lesbian is political, but still I live with an internal dialogue about the virtues of sitting in my room hunched over my computer, rather than going to meetings and demonstrations and doing volunteer work in the lesbian community.

Writing gives me more joy and satisfaction than anything else I have ever done. Writing also gives me a great deal of grief and anxiety. Sometimes I think I should give it all up, get a well-paid full-time job with a dental plan and a pension plan and save money for my old age.

For many years I agonized over whether or not to have a child. I worried that it would be too difficult to balance both a child and writing with the rest of my life. I kept postponing the decision until I finally accepted that I could not have everything I wanted in my life.

Almost everything comes before my writing. I feel I must wash the breakfast dishes and put in a load of laundry and pay the phone bill before I can start writing in the morning. And I interrupt my writing to shop for groceries and take phone calls from friends and do waged work. When friends or family come to visit, I abandon my writing entirely.

I yearn to give up my waged work for a while and concentrate solely on writing. I wonder, year after year, does the Canada Council reject my applications for writing grants because I am a lesbian writer? Because I am a woman writer? Because my writing is not good enough? Because the federal and provincial governments make sure there is not enough money for all the worthy but needy writers in this country?

Still, I never forget that I am privileged to live in Canada. In some parts of this world I would not be able to publish my lesbian writing. In some countries I would be imprisoned. In a few places I would be executed.

I hope, through my writing, I am contributing something to our movements to radically change ourselves and the world.

Class and Race

In the 1970s the active feminists (who were mostly lesbians in my community) talked about sisterhood and were concerned about women's issues — sexism, safe and legal abortions, child care, equal pay for work of equal value, rape and other forms of violence against women. A few of us were also concerned with issues we called gay rights, such as custody rights for lesbian mothers and including sexual orientation in the Human Rights Act.

In the 1980s we finally began to recognize some other vital issues for women, especially race and class.

I am a white woman and I am especially aware of my white privilege in the all-important world of waged employment. In 1984 and 1985 I worked for a local agency that provides services for immigrants and refugees. Out of a staff of fourteen women and men, three of us were white Anglos. As soon as I walked in the room I understood it is no accident that I have worked with white people for years. And I soon realized that when there is even a little will to hire people from diverse cultures and races, it can be done easily. (Of course, I learned much more than this from working with people from four continents.)

Since then, I have worked for a few national non-profit groups concerned with social issues. The people who make decisions about hiring are always white and I work (with only one exception) with white people. I believe this is not an accident and seems to come, as far as I can tell, from very subtle racist attitudes — especially since these organizations have personnel policies which forbid any kind of discrimination.

I live in a country of rampant and deeply ingrained racism. I have to watch myself closely because I am not always aware of my own racism. In a story that was published in 1987, a character says "decked out in full war paint" to describe the makeup her daughter is wearing. I think makeup is part of the undeclared war between women and men. A small voice in my head kept asking if aboriginal people would find the reference amusing or offensive. I rewrote that passage to remove that line before the story was published again in 1990.

I called myself a feminist for more than ten years before I became consciously aware of class. In my family we pretended we were middle class, although my mother was working in a spinning mill and my father in a furniture factory when they met in 1947.

A few years ago I watched a well-known Canadian pollster being interviewed on TV. He said that 96 per cent of Canadians say they are middle class. This is, as he said himself, impossible. A lot of us believe we are middle class, if we think about it at all, even when our lives do not match the middle-class movies and TV shows we watch.

Now I am almost constantly aware of class, yet I have trouble writing about it. I started an essay on class in 1986 but have never been able to finish it — although working on it has helped me to recognize that I usually pass for middle class. (I used to pass for straight a lot, too, but in recent years I don't seem to much. I wonder, have I become more blatantly dykey as I age?)

Another issue for women that I think we have been slow to recognize is poverty. I have been one of the working poor for most of my adult life. My companion is also from a white working-class family. I am amazed at the lives we have managed to create for ourselves in the last few years. I make very little money as a writer and working part-time at other jobs, but I am able to live in comfort, thanks to a gift from my parents, as well as the combined money my companion and I earn.

In the early 1990s I worked for a national anti-poverty group. Job applicants were usually asked if they had any personal experience with poverty. I was repeatedly astonished by their replies and had to keep telling myself, Yes, Candis, there are people who have never ever been poor.

Racism. Homophobia. The words of fear and hate that hurt me most are those I hear within my family. I refuse to listen any more.

The more I talk and write about poverty and class and race, the more I learn to think and see beyond my working/middle-class and Celtic/Scottish/WASP whiteness. Working on these revolutionary issues is essential as we change the world.

More Change

In the 1990s I occasionally do volunteer work for community events, but mostly I focus on my writing, my relationships and my health and the impact of my actions.

I am learning to create a truly loving relationship, an intimacy based on trust, openness and empathy, with my companion, Wendy Clouthier. After years with her, I think I am finally beginning to learn to love in a healthy way. I wish I could say how we have achieved this fulfilling and oh so satisfying intimacy — but I don't know. I have noticed that we are less selfish and tend to compromise more in recent years. I feel safe with her. I believe she loves me. When I withdraw, she comes to me and gathers me in her arms. But surely there is more than that.

I would not want anyone to think that we have achieved the ideal intimate relationship. I have been known to say, "The first seven years were pure hell." And we still have some horribly rough times.

We encourage each other to take our body's needs seriously, giving up smoking in August 1991 (after twenty-four years of addiction for me and eighteen for Wendy) and gradually eliminating meat and other toxins from our diets. Wendy has given up sugar and caffeine entirely. We cook and bake with unsweetened concentrated fruit juices and maple syrup, although I still enjoy white sugar when I indulge in my two cups of black tea each day.

We recycle and reuse and compost. We live in the country and garbage is not picked up in our township so we take our refuse to the local "landfill site" every few weeks — along with boxes of newspaper and tins and glass to be recycled. We collect plastic, too, but haven't found a place to recycle it yet. We pass used clothes and furniture to family and friends. Every few months we take office paper to Ottawa and pay $10 plus 7 per cent GST per barrel to have it recycled.

We are learning how to grow food and flowers, and how to care for trees and the land without using chemical insecticides, pesticides and fertilizers. Our lawnmower mulches the grass as it cuts it and then spreads it back over the lawn. Inside the house we use biodegradable dish soap, clothes detergent and other cleaning products. We have a few cloth shopping bags, which has really cut down on our use of plastic and paper bags. We try to support artists and small businesses, health food stores and farmers' markets rather than large corporations and chain stores. We talk of bartering but haven't done that yet.

It is a process of change and we have much to learn. For example, we still use plastic bags to collect our garbage.

For twenty years I have been learning to live my life differently from the way I was brought up and the ways I see on television and in the shopping malls. Everyday I am learning to resist, to be disobedient, to stand up for myself and others, to think about what I am doing and what it means to me and to other women. I am learning to love myself. I am trying, slowly but surely, to transform myself.

Afterthoughts

Sometimes I learn because someone else suffers horribly. In 1990 a friend was brutally raped. I had started a new story some days before the rape and afterwards, when I could write again, I found the story was changing. The violent rape and my emotional response to it helped focus some of my beliefs and values, and brought them into my fiction. This is from that story, "Imperfect Moments."

> ... the reason our mothers give birth to us and the reason we populate this earth is not to accumulate possessions or acquire riches or assume power over the lives of others. We are here to be with each other. What other reason could there be than to share our pleasures and

sorrows, to hold and be held, to tend the small hurts and the large ones, to celebrate together, to seek each other out with gentle hearts and open minds and loving hands ... we are here to be true and loyal to each other all our lives ... not only to live with compassion for one another for as many years as we have in this world but also to honour this planet as much as we honour our selves.

It is a life-long struggle.

My (Lesbian) Breast Cancer Story: Can I Get a Witness?

Kathleen Martindale

> Bearing witness to a trauma is, in fact, a process that includes the listener. For the testimonial process to take place, there needs to be a bonding, the intimate and total presence of an *other* — in the position of one who hears. Testimonies are not monologues; they cannot take place in solitude. The witnesses are talking *to somebody:* to somebody they have been waiting for a long time.
>
> Dori Laub,
> *Testimony: Crises in Witnessing in Literature, Psychoanalysis and History* [1]

Part 1: Joining the Cancer Club

It happened to me the way it does to most women. I found the lump in my breast myself. It hurt and that saved my life. This is my story of how I joined the Cancer Club. Among other things, it's a lesbian story. I particularly, but not exclusively, address it to other lesbians, not so much to scare you or make you upset, but to move you to anger and action.

Cancer is bad enough, but the homophobia which goes along with most forms of thinking about and treating breast cancer is as devastating as it is unnecessary.

Based on my experiences and my reading of the literature handed out in hospital waiting rooms, as well as of many autobiographical narratives by breast cancer survivors of diverse sexual orientations, I believe that the very mode of understanding the disease, its treatment and its consequences for those who suffer from it, has been heterosexualized. By that I mean that breast cancer is framed overwhelmingly as a crisis in and for heterosexuality. Breast surgery is regarded as a symbolic assault on a woman's femininity and, hence, her value in heterosexual terms. The literature I was given and which is displayed in radiation and chemotherapy waiting rooms doesn't mention the medical or other existential dilemmas women with breast cancer face — it deals with how to use makeup, wigs, scarves, turbans and prostheses to hide the disease and how to pass for normal. Lesbians, as well as other women who refuse or are unable to pass for normal, are devalued and unintelligible in terms of the dominant culture's handling of breast cancer and can expect homophobic reactions if they "act up."

For the first six months after diagnosis, I had the usual treatments that women who are lucky enough to be Canadian, white, and living above the poverty line in large cities get when they've got early-stage breast cancer. I had a lumpectomy in January of 1992; then radiation for six weeks; then six months of chemotherapy began. The lumpectomy was nothing compared to the other treatments. For one thing, it's over quickly and you're unconscious. It's downhill from there.

Getting radiated was the real beginning of the nightmare

for me. For early-stage cancer patients, the treatments seem worse than the disease. Because there are so many cancer patients and not enough technicians or machines, access is an issue, but patients are not told why the system is in crisis and complaining is futile. Some women with breast cancer are sent hundreds of miles away from Toronto for the duration of their treatments.

If you're lucky enough to be treated where you live, as I was, you have no control over the time your daily appointments will take place. They could happen anytime between 9:00 a.m. and 5:00 p.m, for approximately six weeks, and you're given no time to plan. Though the treatment itself took only five minutes, the wait was usually over an hour. Many working people risk losing their jobs or have to go on disability under these conditions, and the anxieties created by missing work or possibly losing a job add enormously to those having cancer itself produces.

Along with the daily visits to the hospital, the experience of radiation transforms you into a patient, literally, ''one who suffers.'' First, you're tattooed in order to mark the areas the machine will hit. Then, the technicians mark the entire area, in my case from the neck down and around the entire breast, with indelible ink. These signs marked me with the signs of my disease. For six weeks, I was forbidden to shower and was yelled at by the technicians when the marks were not visible enough. Because my tattooed and semi-naked body was tied down in a vulnerable position, exposed to an ever-changing group of technicians who roughly manipulated my breast, shoulder and arms and otherwise treated me like a thing, the radiation room called up associations to the gas chambers.

The brutality of many of the technicians encouraged these thoughts. One male technician herded me in, pushing me from behind. When the machine is set, the technicians run out, locking the special thick doors that protect them — the healthy — from the sick, the radiated. Once safely outside the chamber, they press the button that sets the machine whining. I'll never forget the sound as it delivered the zap to my immobilized tattooed body.

Radiation may or may not help prevent recurrences of cancer, and it may actually cause other cancers, but it is quite effective at turning you into a cancer patient. The cancer establishment, and in my experience, that most definitely includes women doctors and technicians, tells you over and over again that "resistance is futile." The first radiologist I saw, a woman, called me a non-cooperator when I asked questions about the treatments. She warned me that bad things would happen to me if I remained militant. After I fired her, I got another female radiologist who laughed when I threatened to complain about the system. Whatever else it does, going to a cancer hospital every weekday for six weeks, under these conditions, is effective at destroying emotional well-being and inducing fear and impotent rage.

If you're lesbian, even in metropolitan Toronto, there's no psychological or social support. There are no organized groups intended for us. All the cancer pamphlets in hospital waiting rooms are written for heterosexual, indeed, married women. The biggest problem for women with mastectomies, according to Cancer Society lore, is the possibility, no, likelihood, that their husbands will leave them or become sexually dysfunctional because "their" woman is mutilated.

The heterosexists who run support groups do not notice that our needs might be different from that of the married middle-class housewives, for whom they design their therapy. My social worker got back to my lover and me on the lesbian question (whether there were any others in the groups, had the leaders ever had lesbians in the groups, would we be treated like a couple) *ten* weeks after we called seeking help. They smugly assured us that, though they had never knowingly had a lesbian with cancer in their groups before, we wouldn't be rejected because this was a big city and the patients were fairly young and therefore "tolerant." We declined, horrified.

The oncologist, another woman, recommended six months of chemotherapy, something they routinely advise for women with early breast cancer. Then she left on maternity leave. My case was passed on to a male oncologist, who turned out to be the only compassionate doctor I encountered. He alone was willing to talk and to listen. He even took me seriously enough to argue about how to interpret a footnote in a medical article. After listening to my complaints about the side effects of the standard chemotherapy regime the first oncologist had ordered, he made adjustments which significantly improved my quality of life. There was, however, no place for him in the leading breast cancer facility in Toronto, so he had to leave.

Chemo was not the nightmare I expected it to be. It was another, and far subtler, one. Each time I went to the hospital for the IV treatments which pumped poisons through my veins, brought on early menopause and destroyed my immune system, I felt as if I was not only desecrating my body, but giving it over to my enemies, the medical establishment. Why, then, did I do it? I felt I had no alternative. For a quarter of a century, I've lived the more socially approved, medically sanctified parts of an "alternative lifestyle" anyhow — I'm a non-smoking, vegetarian, marathon runner who meditates, does yoga, occasionally even succumbs to thinking positive thoughts, and, I got cancer.

I was heavily invested in doing chemo "well." I read the

Bernie Siegel books. I tried to imagine the chemo drugs as healing energies, if not precisely the "white knights" he recommends (they made me think of the Ku Klux Klan), but this is as easy to believe as that cops are my friends and that "family values" are good for women and children. The chemo drugs may have been killing cancer cells, but that didn't make them my buddies. I saw the months of chemo as some kind of ultra-marathon. The key was to endure and not ask why you're doing it in the first place.

Doing chemo well meant not heaving my guts out, and in that limited sense, I guess I did do well. I never vomited, but I had "background nausea" two weeks out of every four and lived in a grey state of terror and weakness for the duration. I lost my appetite, a lot of weight and most of my hair. What remained had the brittle and fragile texture of corn silk. We called it "chemo hair." On the regime most often prescribed for early breast cancer, which the chemo nurses jokingly call "baby chemo" — because it's "so mild" in its side-effects compared to other chemotherapy cocktails — my skin became greenish and my entire respiratory system and digestive tract, from end to end, became a war zone. My mouth was full of sores, I had severe bronchitis, a bout of pneumonia, constipation so bad it made me weep and shake when I visited the toilet. I moved and looked as if I were thirty years older. The chemo unit was proud of having a full-time pharmacist attached to it who was supposed to answer questions about side-effects. When the bronchitis attacked me so severely I couldn't sleep or move, she denied that it had anything to do with the drugs I was prescribed, although the *Physicians Desk Reference* and other standard reference works indicate that bronchitis and all the other symptoms I had are typical effects of the chemo regime used on me. Chemotherapy may have increased my chances of survival by nine or so per cent, but I experienced it as a life-rupturing voyage, a pre-figurement of my own dying, a period of prolonged, and yet anticipatory, mourning.

As well as the IV drugs, I took three nitrogen mustard-like pills (the stuff they use in chemical warfare) every two weeks out of four until the second oncologist changed the delivery system. I'd meditate before taking them in order to psych myself up for the self-poisoning. I never lost the feeling of profound conflict about what I was doing to myself. Of course, you don't know whether chemotheraphy has worked until you have a recurrence, then, as with the other cancer treatments, you know it hasn't.

In mid-July, half way through chemo, my progress through the cancer pipeline hit a snag. The radiation doctor thought I had grown more cancerous lumps. She consulted with the surgeon who stupidly did a needle biopsy first, which made it impossible to do a mammogram at the same time. I had to wait ten days more for that. Even before all the results were in, she told me that she had bad news. The biopsy indicated the presence of cancer cells. She examined me to see how much she'd have to cut. She estimated thirty per cent of my right breast was filled with lumps. Doing another lumpectomy wasn't wise. This time, it had to be a mastectomy. Because she was going away on holidays, I would have to wait with the time-bomb ticking inside me for three weeks. She dismissed me.

If, in the months from January to mid-July, life had seemed tough, nothing prepared me for life-after-recurrence fever. I had been seeing a female therapist who specialized in cancer. She abandoned me to go on her holidays and left no back-up. She charged $120 for 50 minutes, which I could only afford because I'm lucky enough to have extensive medical coverage. I tried to get a second opinion. Having cancer is bad enough at any time, but it's definitely not smart to have it in August when most surgeons are on holidays and the ones who are around are very, very busy, since this is an epidemic. When the lump became painful, I pleaded with the oncologist to have another surgeon examine me. The new one did, without looking at my recent records; he assured me that everything was fine. The tumour would not metastasize during the delay. There was nothing to worry about. He dismissed me.

On September 2, 1992, I had a bilateral mastectomy. It turned out that I did not need to have my breasts cut off. I hadn't had a recurrence. During the surgery, but after the cutting, the first pathology reports came back negative. No sign of cancer. By then, of course, it was too late. My surgeon told this to me when I was coming out of the anaesthetic. Since my lover thought I was hallucinating, she asked the surgeon to repeat what she had said. A bit shamefaced, she repeated what I thought I had heard the first time. A week or so later, when all the results came back, there was still no sign of cancer.

Why did my very senior and very experienced surgeon goof? Doctors don't like explaining the little boo-boos they make and surgeons in particular are known for not being talkative. She was a little vague, and all my questions led nowhere, especially not to clear explanations, let alone apologies. I remembered what I had said to the radiologist who warned me not to be a non-cooperator: "how do you sleep at night?" I can only conjecture that the needle biopsy was a false positive. Probably my surgeon shouldn't have gone ahead with the mastectomies on the basis of that one test, not only because (as anyone familiar with breast cancer knows) cancer cells are very frequently present in non-cancerous breast tissue, but interpreting needle biopsies or mammograms performed on radiated breasts is about as conclusively scientific as reading tea leaves.

Was it bad medicine or no medicine at all? What I learned from having had an unnecessary bilateral mastectomy is how much doctors do not know about breast cancer and how unwise it is to trust them. My surgeon probably was going more on intuition and years of slashing rather than anything that could be called "scientific" evidence in determining that my new lump was cancerous and that my entire breast needed to be amputated. (My oncologist, the one who couldn't get a permanent job in the same centre, has told me that *he* learned something from my tragedy: on at least one occasion, he intervened in another woman's case and so a biopsy was done, a suspicious lump that turned out not to be cancerous was removed, and a mastectomy was prevented.)

When I tried to learn the logic under which the surgeon acted, she evaded answering directly. Looked at one way, I have had good luck. Cancer hadn't come back, at least not that time. Though she didn't say it explicitly, I was aware that breast cancer should probably be regarded as a chronic disease. That means there's no remission time after which you can breathe a sigh of relief and know that you're cured. She was a bit bashful when she admitted that the surgery had been unnecessary, but she followed it up by drawing a diagram of how she teaches medical students about mortality statistics. She ended our interview by telling me what she tells her medical students: in the long run we all die. Thank you, doctor!

Do I have grounds for suing? Probably not. Wilfully not knowing is the name of the game with breast cancer. I've got an invisible disability. I've become a quick-change artist in gyms and other places where there's little privacy. Most people cringe when they see my chest. They say I've been mutilated. In place of breasts with nipples, I have a scar which extends from under my left armpit, goes jaggedly across my entire body, and then ends up under what used to be my right armpit. My lover and I call it "the zipper." That's what it looks like, a long red zipper across my puckered torso.

Part 2: Lesbian Breast Cancer Narratives: Not Just a Fashion Problem

Does the world really need another cancer narrative? There are far too many already. But, in a cultural climate where even implicitly feminist discourses about breast cancer such as *Dr. Susan Love's Breast Book* are still ignored by both the medical cancer establishment and the very popular new age self-help counter-establishment which smugly blames victims and gets away with it, lesbian testimonials to the experiences of multiple stigmatization that those of us with breast cancer face are completely tuned out.

And so I see myself as writing in what is becoming a tradition, that of the lesbian crying in the wilderness, attempting to reach other lesbians to warn them about this epidemic. Act up or it might be your turn next. As Sandra Butler puts it, in the introduction to *Cancer in Two Voices,* quoting Barbara Rosenblum, her lover, who was misdiagnosed and ultimately died of metastatic cancer caused by medical malpractice, " Many of my friends will see their future in the way I handle mine. There will be others. It's only a matter of time."[2]

The most moving and analytical narratives about breast cancer have been written by lesbians: Audre Lorde's *The Cancer Journals* and Sandra Butler and Barbara Rosenblum's *Cancer in Two Voices.* But you won't find these testimonies in the waiting rooms of cancer clinics.

I think there are two reasons why no one's listening to lesbians who write about breast cancer. One is that since lesbians are treated even worse than straight women by the cancer establishment, we don't tend to be as grateful about the torture they dish out. The other is that lesbians seem to have a different attitude about breast cancer from most heterosexual women: we insist that breast cancer is happening to us, to our bodies, to our lives. It is not primarily about men's reactions to us, whether they'll leave us or whether we won't be able to find a man who will accept our surgically altered bodies.

In other words, based on what I've seen, heard and read, I suspect that for lesbians, breast cancer is primarily an issue of their own survival, rather than a crisis for heterosexual men or for their kids, and this view makes our reactions to our own cancer seem "militant." Consider the television and press coverage of the first Canadian conference on breast cancer, held in Montreal in the fall of 1993, and organized by survivors. The *one* voice that was chosen to represent all the speakers at the conference was a man's. Breast cancer, such imagery suggests, is a tragedy because he lost a wife and his child lost a mother. What such framing of breast cancer ignores or at the very least downplays — is the loss of women's health and lives.

According to the same homophobic logic, breast cancer is turned into a fashion problem. Non- or anti-feminist cancer literature is upbeat; my favourite is a wacky pamphlet you can find in any chemotherapy waiting room. It's called *Looking Good, Feeling Better.* It teaches women undergoing chemo how to disguise their baldness under turbans and scarves. Cancer narratives written by straight women pick up this theme. Though they are full of tragi-comic anecdotes about medical incompetence, the real centre of their stories are the accepting or rejecting reactions of their husbands and boyfriends, the major players in their lives. Though quietly heroic in their fight against both the disease and the doctors who mistreat it and them, they do not tend to think in terms of mounting a collective analysis or struggle against both. Lesbian and feminist narratives do, and for that they reason they are both more angry and more political. They are, therefore, more likely to be marginalized in both official (medical and self-help) discourses on breast cancer. Thus, I write, adding my voice to what I hope will become a din which can't be ignored.

Let's say you've just been diagnosed, or a friend has, and you want to know what you can expect. You might have the misfortune to find *Women Talk About Breast Surgery: From Diagnosis to Recovery.* This scary book, edited by two female dolts, suggests what lesbians are likely to be up against. The book is relentlessly positive, but I see from glancing at the book as I write this that they already edited *Women Talk About Gynecological Surgery,* so they've got a good thing going. As long as women have "female troubles," they're in business.

Amy Gross and Dee Ito interviewed a bunch of middle-class women, almost all of whom were white and straight, who are breast cancer survivors. These privileged women are their models of the "new patient" who fights the medical establishment — and wins! The editors claim that the cancer experience is very manageable if you, the patient, take charge. This is a deadly fantasy, not the least of all because it disguises the editors' racist, classist, sexist and homophobic agenda.

Like me, their interviewees read all they can and became

experts on their disease. Like the good girls they are, they insist that errors they have made — bad diets and too much stress — caused their illness, rather than environmental pollution or just some unknown combination of genes, pollution, lifestyle and bad luck. Unlike me, everything goes well for them. Not so coincidentally, none of the women has metastatic cancer or a "bad" prognosis. There's an endorsement from socialist feminist Barbara Ehrenreich on the front cover. Why'd she do it?

After mastectomies, all these happy heterosexuals had reconstructive plastic surgery to give them back the boobs that society and their hubbies and boyfriends craved. Breast reconstruction is expensive and involves a lengthy series of painful operations, in which expanders are put under the skin on the chest wall, and then foreign substances, some known to be carcinogenic, are implanted. The implants make it more difficult to detect recurrences. Skin is grafted from other parts of the body to make new mounds. Sometimes simulated nipples are created, too, through the use of dyes or tattooing. Unsafe, probably; ridiculous, maybe; heterosexist, surely.

Although I'm pretty used to reading medical atrocity stories by now, descriptions of breast reconstruction are not for the faint of stomach. All of these obvious objections to them are, however, finessed by Gross and Ito. According to them and their interviewees, deciding to have a reconstruction is a sign of having a positive body image post-mastectomy. Run that logic by me again! Of course, the surgeons stress that the mastectomies (that's what they call us) should have a "realistic" attitude about what these fake boobs will look like. That is, you get "half a grapefruit," with scars. A feminist analysis of all this never occurs to these women and their medical establishment-friendly editors.

Gross and Ito's manufactured happy endings are nothing like the tragic story of the medical negligence which killed lesbian academic Barbara Rosenblum, as lovingly, if harrowingly recounted, in diary form by her lover, Sandra Butler, in *Cancer in Two Voices.* It's more than a cancer narrative; it's a lesbian love story. Nor could Gross and Ito, or any of the medical establishment they pimp for, allow in their book a hint of the political analysis of the ugly combination of breast fetishism/mammary-directed heterosexism that Audre Lorde produced in *The Cancer Journals.*

Did I mourn for my breasts? No, not exactly. I was afraid they were killing me. I wanted them gone. A gay male colleague suggested that this wouldn't be as hard for me as for a het woman. People (who can't get breast cancer) say the funniest things. "Them," that's right. Did I, the articulate, militant feminist academic, fail to be the informed, assertive "new patient"? Or is what happened to me just typical of women's fate at the hands of the cancer establishment? You be the judge. Meanwhile, I've still got problems thinking those positive thoughts about Bernie Siegel's "white knights" of chemo and asking myself why I *chose* to get cancer, why so many of my friends *chose* to get AIDS, and we all *choose,* even the most positive thinkers among us, to get...dead. Like they say, don't mourn, organize. Or even better, mourn and organize.

Endnotes

1. Shoshana Felman and Dori Laub, *Testimony: Crises in Witnessing In Literature, Psychoanalysis and History* (New York: Routledge, 1992), 71-72.
2. Sandra Butler and Barbara Rosenblum, *Cancer in Two Voices* (San Francisco: Spinsters, 1991), i.

Jane & Jane
Are Not the Same

Betsy Warland

Dick and Jane: our first institutionalized role models for many of us growing up in the fifties. Gendered givens not only for blond, blue-eyed, middle-class north americans like me, but for most kids — the education system indifferent to the Dicks and Janes of other races, classes or cultures. It's notable that in this standard reader the boy was named Dick, considering the vast array of names to select from. And the girl — just a plain Jane. No worries though, it's nothing that a Dick couldn't fix. Spot (the dog) and Puff (the cat), clear name indicators of the relevance of the natural world in that decade. "Read, ar-, To fit together." So many lives scripted by these innocent names.

Penetrate, *penitus*, deeply from *penus*, the interior of a house: first meaning listed — to enter or force a way into; pierce."

"Permeate, *per-*, through + *meare*, to go, pass: first meaning listed — to spread or flow through."

Jane & Jane weren't even a possibility in post-war, baby-boom north america. Aside from social and religious taboos, there was (and still is) the general attitude: "what could two women *do?*" In the absence of Dick, lesbian lovemaking seems pointless. Ironically, in this very pointlessness there is freedom to discover pleasures previously unconsidered in heterosexual sex. With lesbian lovemaking, everything can be of value; everything can be renewed. The whole-body focus of most lesbian lovers, as contrasted to site-specific heterosexual lovemaking, encourages an unpredicktable eroticism. When the entire body is erotically electrified, current charges and *permeates* in countless directions; roles and bodies are in constant motion.

But what about fist fucking, dildos, the powerful sensation of parthenogenesis and tribadism? These can be related to penetration, yet tend not to eclipse other ways of making love, as the penis often does with its institutionalized, economic superiority.

Lesbian-lover relationships are generally not economically determined relationships. Heterosexual relationships are the foundation of the economy: weddings, divorces, child support agreements, private property, consumer and cultural industries, life insurance, legal council and judicial activity are essential economic activities generated from this coupling. The *(hetero)sexualizing of the environment* is rooted in a phallic proprietary economy.

Lesbian couples generate economic activity, but we're often poor consumers. As women, our couples' and families' earning power is frequently limited. Our average couple income is often considerably less than heterosexual couples of similar class, race, ethnicity, (or, for that matter, gay male couples not depleted by AIDS). We nearly always insist on financial independence, are typically responsible for our own income, and maintain our own bank accounts. We help each other out when in need and have some shared ownership, but joint accounts are not the norm.

Yet, more lesbians have relatively well-paid jobs than twenty years ago. More have managed to accumulate some money over the years through savings. Some older and wealthier lesbians have received portions of family inheritance. Still, our need to be self-directed and not dependent on someone else's money and values runs deep.

The lesbian body (communal) differs from the heterosexual body (communal) because the only "skin" that bonds us is the skin of desire. In gatherings of various communal lesbian bodies, we can experience sensual significance of all our disparate "members," just as we give ourselves erotically to the entirety of our lover's body and our own body when making love. As lesbian-feminists, we *sensualize the environment* creating an "economy, *oikos*, house + *-nomos*, managing" of intimate pleasures. This is the very source of the joy which nourishes and sustains us within a homophobic, decidedly hostile world.

At a predominantly lesbian party, concert, conference, meeting or bar, we are energized by the sensual energy of *our collective body*. As we move *into and with this body* of women we would like to know, women with whom we enjoy the emotional sensuality of friendship, women with whom we have been lovers and often continue to experience an intimate knowingness of, a woman/women with whom we are lovers, women we may never know but nevertheless feel the energy of, and a woman/women we are or have been in conflict with, yet who also contribute to the current, we are continually recharged.

You can feel it, even in the simple gesture of greeting. When a lesbian embraces someone with affection, she usually responds with her whole body. She gives a full-body hug, not a pyramid hug — where only the upper parts of our bodies are allowed to touch. As lesbians, our entire body is erotic: our sexuality isn't deposited in one loaded zone that must be avoided.

Coupling is important, but the communal — as I have

described above — is possibly more important, because it generates contexts for our loving which would otherwise be non-existent. Unlike gay men who can find many of their values and images reflected in commercial and cultural norms, many of us must imagine and make our own, affirming social context. Given the wide spectrum of disparate racial, social, political and spiritual lives in lesbian communities, coupled with our extremely limited access to occupying safe public space, the intensity of the collective bodies we generate is all the more potent. This can energize and frighten us.

Many dykes, queers and lesbians live on their own. Occasionally, they are involved in a lover relationship, often they are not. Unlike heterosexual "single" women who are too often riddled with despair, self-doubt, and judged as inadequate by their community, the ontoherself lesbian is a vibrant part of our communal body. Yet, it's not unusual to hear complaints about "coupledom" in our community. As women, we are socialized and possibly biologically inclined (being the birth-givers) to the domestic, to a sense of family, to the enjoyment of daily affection, and tend to associate with other lesbians who have shaped their lives similarly. It must also be acknowledged, however, that the underlying fears of intrusion are unfortunately once again at play, just as with heterosexual couples. Contrary to Noah, everything doesn't come in pairs.

Though an ontoherself lesbian is respected and valued within the communal body, she's not automatically socially included. Perhaps, even more frustrating, she must spend time with her friends in their tandems too frequently. This blending seriously limits our friendships. It also slowly muffles the erotic energy between lovers. Distrust of difference threatens our intimacies far more than the other woman.

By rejecting the ideal of universality, which easily can become a tool of oppression and privilege, we-the-not-all lesbians of the Jane generation can subscribe to the practice of difference. Since the Jane generation has played a significant role in shaping lesbian sensibilities (the political, the emotional, the cultural), our modus operandi has imprinted lesbians from other generations, as well as other social, political and racial origins. This has caused a lot of problems within our increasingly diverse communities. Fortunately, many of these one-sided, simplistic sensibilities are shifting or sinking, while others seem shared enough to embrace through dissimilarities.

With the valuing of difference, do we become communities whose only bond is in how we make love? [Even here, as with feminism, we have deep differences regarding S/M.] Or, might lesbians be attempting to develop a new kind of *apartness* shaped not only by sexual identity and feminism but by our specific difference? An *apartness* in which we find pleasure in being *apart* (alone and different) as well as in being *part of* (together and different)?

Contrasted to heterosexual relationships, whose power is ascribed to *the discovery of sameness within difference*, lesbians' power is located in *the discovery of difference within our illusory sameness.* This is a radical shift, not only in viewing intimacy but also in viewing the world. We Jane-lesbian-feminists are just beginning to throw off the patriarchal tenet that all women are alike. This is a profound patriarchal strategy which has utterly determined our very aptitude for perception about the differences among ourselves. Jane & Jane are not the same, just because they haven't a Dick!

One of the most often cited problems within lesbian-lover relationships is symbiosis; eroticism and sensuality are repeatedly choked out by the prizing of similarities. Joyce P. Lindenbaum was among the first feminists to examine intimacy dynamics which seemed specific to lesbian couples. In her 1985 essay, "The Shattering of an Illusion: The Problem of Competition in Lesbian Relationships," Lindenbaum wrote:

> Because they [the lesbian couple] are both women, it is easier for them to identify with each other, to empathize, to believe that one knows what the other feels.... Eventually the couple sacrifices sex. They do this because the merging has become too intense, too overwhelming, and the loss of self is too catastrophic. They do it because the memory of a long-forgotten time in earliest childhood has been stirred, and the pain of loss is too great.... The longed-for merger, then, is created in the nonsexual aspect of the relationship. It...is preserved not by the power of sexual union or the mutual connection of two separate people, but by fear of differentiation.[1]

Lindenbaum goes on to say that most often lesbian couples separate "in the name of difference," yet their "relationship ends precisely because so few real differences have been allowed to exist." The need to feel safe? "Safe, *Slang.* A condom" or "A metal container usually having a lock, used for storing valuables; strongbox." "Without risk"? This is the antithesis of what it means to be a lesbian in a Mr. & Mrs. World.

Dominant lesbian-feminist communities have begun to seriously confront fears of difference. Perhaps this will also occur within our beliefs about intimacy. As lesbian communities become more and more diverse, encounters with racism, classism, ageism and ableism reach down into our guts, deep into our consciousness. In the communities I know, this is generating a greater urgency than ever before; a far more felt necessity to recognize and respect difference. The well-being, the very possibility of our collective communal body absolutely hinges on it.

Differences within heterosexual relationships are romanticized, trivialized or resented. As lesbians, it is crucial that we do not thoughtlessly adopt these responses as lovers or as close friends. Heterosexual women can readily locate difference within the significant men in their lives, but how do we acknowledge it within ourselves as women? Especially in relationships that do not embody obvious differences of race, culture, class, age, ability, etc. And in relationships that do embody obvious difference, do those differences become the magnets for registering dissimilarity and conflict while assumptions of our sameness as women remain intact? Quietly sabotaging our trust?

If, as lovers and friends, we do recognize the *differences within our illusory sameness*, we'll no longer interact (or react) only within the confines of polarity thinking (if she is right about this, then I must be wrong/ if she wants more independence in our relationship, then she's not in love with me any more). The mutual discovery of our differences will ensure the health of our intimacy (lovers are no longer stuck in fixed roles — both are in motion and both are actively engaged in the evolutionary process of reshaping their relationship as they go). Griselda Pollock's notion of "co-emergence" may also be applicable to this process.[2]

We can then recognize when our desire (based on the pursuit of sameness) goes awry, when it has converted into a will for control and finiteness. Fusion fuelled by fear. Desire based on the pursuit of difference is desire for a revelatory ongoing encounter; is desire nourished by in*her*-ent curiosity, not always anticipating the comfort of illusory sameness; is desire which doesn't immediately resort to feelings of betrayal when differences inevitably arise. This openness requires self-knowledge on each of our parts; possibly a new language of emotions which clearly signals our fears of difference and our profound need for respect. Without it, we will inevitably remain threatened.

As lesbians we know that no four breasts are the same, no two bums or cunt smells, no four labia, lips or hands.

I suspect that many of us need to shake ourselves out of the complacency of the first model for couple intimacy: Mom and Dad. It's crucial that we refuse to be seduced by infantilism of our love to the pre-erotic "safe" state of childhood affection. These nuclear family models prevent the maturation of our culture at every turn.

Are we ourselves afraid of our own revolutionary nature? Do heterosexual models seduce us because of their reassuring familiarity? Seduce. Sedate. And silence us. *Who* are we? Are we adolescent girls secretly playing with each other's bodies within the framework of our Father's House? Or are we unbrid(l)ed women who are "out" to change the world?

We are lesbians. Not familiar. Not safe. Dangerous. With our joyful passion we endlessly renew ourselves. As we meet and embrace our fears of difference — our culture will erupt with a creative force that will shock even us, for a lesbian is a woman who risks everything for love.

Endnotes

1. Joyce P. Lindenbaum, "The Shattering of an Illusion: The Problem of Competition in Lesbian Relationships," *Feminist Studies* 11, no. 1 (Spring 1985): 96-97.
2. Griselda Pollock, public lecture, "Strategies of Dissonance," The Mendel Art Gallery, Saskatoon, Sask., May 6, 1994.

I wish to thank the other voices who are in subtextual conversation with me here: Gloria Anzaldua, Nicole Brossard, Annette Clough, Luce Irigaray, Ottie Lockey, Audre Lorde, Sky Lee, Lee Maracle, Daphne Marlatt, Janet Rogers and Lise Weil.

Pure Electric Energy

Lori Lyons

Teenage lovers do it. Husbands and wives do it. Fathers do it with their children, and so do mothers. Evangelists do it in groups on TV. Rosy-cheeked ceramic children do it in sentimental poses that entice china shop customers. An innocuous sign of affection and unity for nearly everyone in this culture, holding hands is, for queers, defiant, courageous and occasionally stupid. For us, it is flaunting our sex lives.

Gay men try to tell me that it is easier for women, that people will think we're just friends or sisters. I've never found it easy, but it has often been exciting, compelling — a flirtatious dance on a dangerous edge. Holding hands with another woman in a public space makes me feel visible, deviant, and in some places, like a target.

I remember the first time I held hands in public with a lesbian lover. It was late, on the subway, after a boozy night of firstlove euphoria. Until then, our touching had been confined to the protective walls of her tiny bachelor apartment and the fleeting dark anonymity between the fire doors of our school. Even through the mellowing influence of alcohol, this felt reckless, brazen. I remember the startled stares of our fellow subway revellers, the sense of being exposed to their judgement and muttered opinions. I remember the adrenaline danger-warning, a biological plea for caution and alert. I remember it as a moment of revelation, a discovery of dyke defiance.

I was always the good girl in my family. My grades were good, my school attendance sterling. My weekend role as a Sunday schoolteacher and youth group leader was the icing on the conventional cake. The twin-teen temptations of alcohol and drugs held only a fleeting allure. Never drawn to the "bad boys," I rarely dated the good ones, a fact that caused little consternation in my teens. I carried the faintly uneasy knowledge that I was not exactly what everyone thought, but the stirring of my internal rebellion remained bottled until that night on the subway.

I have always rejected the notion that being a lesbian is a lifestyle. It is in fact a fundamental characteristic of my identity, as intrinsic to my person as being a woman. Being visible is another matter. While there have been many times when I have not been brave, when I have demurred and taken the easy way out, public and defiant lesbianism has been my lifestyle of choice since that first tentative taste on a late-night subway. I have led angry chants through city streets until my voice was nearly inaudible. I have talked with reporters, politicians, clerics. I have spoken and written about my sexuality and exchanged steamy embraces with other rebellious dykes, primarily for the benefit of rolling cameras. All these activities have their joys and fears, but none, for me, carries the simple rebellious power of walking along crowded streets, hand in hand with a lover.

Holding hands with a lover or close friend is an unusual combination of politics and intimacy, a modern dyke's actualization of the 1970s feminist motto "The personal is political." It feels natural; it proclaims deviance. Holding hands in a public space is queer activism without the protection of a large group of protesters. It sometimes entails real physical danger, and often requires confronting the reality of heterosexual hostility. It is not always safe, and it is not always fun. It means putting yourself and someone you care about at risk. I have been screamed at, spat at, and, of course, stared at. Others have faced far more serious attacks. As innocuous as our behaviour may seem, we are claiming the heterosexual privilege of public affection and along with it a confrontational familiarity. We are making the politics of lesbian visibility very personal.

Holding hands forces straights who would rather ignore our existence to face lesbians as real people. We are not a screaming mob flashing by on the TV news (although we can be); we are people that walk and shop and laugh on a fine afternoon, strolling with our friends and lovers. Holding hands puts lesbian lives and lesbian sex in the realm of the ordinary, the possible. Walking hand in hand anywhere, anytime, as we go about our lives, frees us from ludicrous and misleading stereotypes, stereotypes who allow many straight people in this country to believe that they have never met a lesbian.

While the political argument for lesbian visibility is compelling, it masks the pure electric energy of queer defiance. Holding hands is a political act, but it is also a sensual one. We are exhibitionists flaunting our desire, our longing and fascination for other women's bodies. Public physical contact, even on the mundane level of hand-holding, suggests that our longing for each other cannot and will not be contained by the disapproval of others — be they straight citizens, children, religious leaders, cops or any of the myriad people we might meet on a public street. When I link my fingers through my lover's, I am entwining myself in fingers that have grasped and pulled at my nipples, that have gently and patiently coaxed my clit to swollen ecstasy. Fingers, now brazenly and publicly merged, that have driven deep into the warm moist interior of the other and now live to advertise the act. We are "flaunting it."

It is my conviction that these intimate rebellions fuel our most effective activism. Sex, desire, defiance are the things that draw us together as a people and as a political force. If we concede our public space, we claim it is only what we do behind closed doors that makes us different. We lose the passion for daring that sustains us in the face of bigotry and ignorance and fuels our fight for a better future. Until public space is our space, queer hands publicly entwined are only the hard-won promise of a better future.

Sliding into Home:
Identifying Lesbian Sex

Judith P.
Stelboum

When I talk about myself as a lesbian I openly declare my sexual preference. I know there are other ways to define lesbian life: social and economic oppression, philosophies, music and literature. But there is one certain aspect of my life that is a constant. The truth of my loving women. Defining myself as a lesbian means declaring myself in a sexual context.

I want to talk about sex because, as a lesbian, I want to exist as an entity in the world. It is not enough for me to be merely tolerated in a heterosexual world. I want my definition of myself as lesbian recognized as a valid identity and as a viable option.

I know this is very dangerous. Forcing people in the straight world to confront what they would rather not know, forcing people to abandon their illusions, can produce hostile reactions. But, we need not look only to the straight world for disdain and anger towards lesbians. We need to look no farther than our own community and its reactions to S/M to understand the enmity and fear directed toward different practices of sex. To affirm our varied existence, we have to learn to risk the dangers of visibility. If we develop and encourage visibility and continue to create and define a lesbian culture, then lesbian identity must become a reality. Though many of us are still individually invisible, we must not remain culturally invisible.

Lesbian identity is a reality. I don't want people thinking that because I have sex with another woman, it's not sex. If I am defined as a non-sexual entity, I don't exist. I don't want someone thinking that sex without a male organ is only a substitute for the real thing. And I don't want any one, lesbian or straight, think that if some of us strap on dildos we want to be men, or that if some of us wear boxer shorts and suits, we really have a secret desire to become male. Lyndall MacCowan states in her article "Recollecting History, Renaming Lives" that "Butch and Femme are lesbian-specific genders, two of many ways to be both a lesbian and a woman. They are unliberated only in the sense that they need liberating from the assumption, made by heterosexuals and lesbian-feminists alike, that they are an imitation of heterosexuality, a clinging to heterosexual femininity or an attempt to masquerade as a man."[1]

Talking about lesbian sexuality frees lesbians from the restrictive, negative concepts which so many of us, for so long, have used to silently construct our lives. These definitions of who we are and why are generally based on what other people told us about ourselves. These dangerous definitions have sabotaged our own efforts at identification. Many lesbians grow up believing these destructive myths and cannot build positive identities or self-esteem. While it is true that it is difficult for lesbians to develop a positive sense of self in the world of the heterosexual majority, writing about sex and open forums and discussions can convert these negative feelings and beliefs.

I have to talk about my sexuality, lesbian sex, because I

don't want to be defined by the psychoanalysts, the American medical association, the local police department, board of education or national sexologists associations. I want to define who I am. I have to know what happens and why I get turned on or off, and how that works with me, for me, and maybe, in a larger sense, for us.

Thinking about the lesbian body, analyzing lesbian sex, reinforces my identity. I don't want my lesbian sexuality to be a mystery, or worse, a joke. Carole S. Vance describes a conference on "sex research" where films were shown depicting heterosexual sex, homosexual sex and lesbian sex. During the conference the word "sex" always referred to heterosexual sex. It did not include homosexual sex nor lesbian sex. Vance says that in the heterosexual films shown "men set the pace and the timing of the activities. Women cooperated. Films showed fellatio but never cunnilingus. All heterosexual films culminated in vaginal penetration. Regarded as 'real sex.' The films of male homosexual sex were highly genital and depicted orgasm.' Vance states that, "in contrast with the films on heterosex and gay men's sex, lesbian sex occurred in a field of daisies, chronicled by discontinuous jump cuts. Sexual activity, never genital, consisted of running in slow motion through sun dappled fields, hand holding, and mutual hair-combing." She explains that these films were considered liberal, and were widely distributed for sex education and counseling.[2]

By denying the powerful sexuality between women, phallocratic cultures keep straight women from exploring a lesbian life, and deny a sexual and, by extension, a real existence to lesbians. It is important, too, that straight women see lesbian life as a viable option because, as we know, not everyone is born lesbian. Women can become lesbians at any stage of their lives. It is essential that more and more women recognize this option to choose. The powerful force of who we are can become a powerful reality in the world.

We must talk about lesbian sex to destroy the myth that heterosex is "normal." We must continue to oppose the assumption of the "normalcy" of female heterosexuality. Many years ago, I heard Dr. Mary Jane Sherfey speak at Vassar College. Someone in the audience asked her to define the most important questions regarding sexuality. She responded by stating that there was really only one important question, and that if we knew the answer most of the questions that we have about human sexuality would be clarified. That single question was, what are the causes of heterosexuality? Everyone was silent for a few seconds and then began to laugh. But she was serious. That question about the nature of female heterosexuality has been discussed many times since then by many writers, including Marilyn Frye, Adrienne Rich and Monique Wittig.

Because of the heterosexist, patriarchal worlds which we inhabit but are not part of, we have never known what is really natural. Moreover, as Sherfey suggested, we can never ever know what is "normal," since the word "normal" basically refers to the majority of the population and should have no value or moral judgement attached to it. In time, we may discover that there is nothing intrinsically, genetically, biologically different between straight women and lesbians. We may find that lesbian sex and lesbian existence is "natural" to women.

Many straight women would rather not know what lesbians do together. This knowledge might seduce them into believing that they, too, would find lesbian sex naturally exciting. Some of our most subtle subjugation comes from our straight female friends. Caught up in society-sanctioned hetero-relationships, they either consciously or un-consciously accept their position, with the lie or rationaliza-tion that they are not attracted to women. "Sexuality is power. The sexual subjugation of women leads to their economic, social and political domination. Lesbians who have no sexual relations with men therefore have an eco-nomic, political and social perspective that goes beyond the male female categories.[3]

In the seventies, men worried about losing their wives, girlfriends to lesbians in consciousness-raising groups. And they were right to worry because that's what happened. For some women it was the strength of feminism, for some women it was the realization of their repressed desires and for others, a political statement became a personal reality. A slogan of the time stated the idea: "feminism is the theory, lesbianism is the practice."

Now, in the nineties, many lesbians have reservations about mainstream feminism. We want more inclusion in health issues, education and the arts. We question whether or not to align ourselves with feminist organizations that continue to ignore us out of their fear of male rejection, be it economic or personal. Many lesbians march for abortion rights but hardly any of our straight female friends march with us at Gay Pride. A few weeks ago, I was watching a program on T.V. about women's issues in the nineties. The panel, chaired by two women well known for their "liberal views" discussed abortion rights, the glass ceiling in busi-ness, women as combat forces in the military, child care for working women, the difficulties of single parents. There was no mention of civil rights for lesbians. No mention of the fight to allow lesbians and gays in the military. Not one single reference to any problems faced in the United States by lesbians. If lesbian problems are not women problems it must be because "lesbians are not women."[4]

But, in the excitement of the seventies, the reality of so many women becoming lesbian did lead to some important questioning. It forced many of the long-held beliefs about lesbians to be reconsidered. Many people, including lesbians, believed that we were created by a bad home life or were helpless victims of our genes. We were not responsible for our own identities, not responsible for our choices to love women. Lesbians were seen as suffering from some dysfunctional psychiatric ailment. We were more to be pitied than condemned. But, as thousands of women, who were at one time heterosexual, made the choice to love other women, biological determination and social upbringing as "causes" for this "perversion" were revealed as inadequate explanations.

Julia Penelope, in her book, *Call Me Lesbian,* states that, "we choose whether or not we will live as who we are. Naming ourselves lesbian is a decision to act on our truest feelings."[5]

And when we act on those true feelings and name ourselves, all of the other names by which society has labeled us become meaningless. If we name ourselves, then we can begin to define ourselves. To discuss what we have in common is to begin the bonding of lesbians to create identities, which truly mirror the varied and various lives which we have created and can create.

In the past several years there has been a growing interest in writing about lesbian sex. These books, fiction and non-fiction, mark an important intellectual, emotional, psychological moment in the process of understanding ourselves and naming ourselves to the world.

Just as there is no one way to be a lesbian, act like a

lesbian, be recognizable as a lesbian, there is no single way to be a sexual lesbian. There is no right or wrong way to have sex. No one way to express lesbian desire. There are no politically correct techniques, acceptable practices that would define in a narrow sense what we call lesbian sex. In fact, the incredible variety of lesbian sexuality is what gives us power. Nor should we want to look upon what we do as in need of categorizing into the labels of acceptable or unacceptable. The more that is known about lesbian sex and desire means more choices in the ways we make love, establish relationships, have sex.

When I talk about lesbian sex, I mean same-sex partner, not same ways of having sex.[6] So we have to begin to talk about aspects of our sexual excitement which are common but not restrictive, descriptive but not proscriptive.

Some lesbians believe that too much emphasis on discussions of sex defines lesbian identity as only sexual. They believe that, while acknowledging our sexual preference, we should concentrate on other aspects of our lives and not allow the straight world to see us only as sex-preferred or sex-obsessed. I disagree. This attitude is a denial of the essential aspect of our lesbian lives. The physical attraction to women is the basis for lesbian identification. It is essential for lesbians to continue to talk about sex, to try to find some common ground which we can recognize when talking about our sexuality.

In a political sense too, it is important to discuss our sexuality with others in an open forum. I really want to answer the question "What do lesbians do?" Because what that question really asks is, "How is it possible to have sex without a penis?" or "How is 'real' sex possible without a man?" We all know this is the assumption behind the question.

I have to answer that important question seriously, in as explicit and clear way as possible. I must talk about lesbian sex if I want recognition. And I have to answer it for us. For all lesbians who still self-hate, who are embarrassed by lesbians who are too overtly dykes, who think that they're somehow superior to other lesbians because of physical attributes, social or professional status. Distinctions between lesbians prevent us from talking about what we do have in common: our love for women and our physical expressions of that love.

Because we live under siege most of the time, we try to protect our vulnerability. We try to pass in so many ways. Some lesbians still believe that their families, co-workers or neighbours would accept us if we didn't call attention to the ways our lives may be different from theirs. Being Jewish, I am conscious of this faulty thinking which allows us to create specious categories of acceptability or unacceptability under the aegis of lesbian. Perhaps some paranoia tempered by history allows me to believe that people who want to hurt us will do it no matter what, and they can hate all of us and each of us. It doesn't matter if you don't own a dildo or watch porno videos, or keep your leather or handcuffs in a trunk. Your femme dress won't save you and neither will your motorcycle jacket. Your professional title won't save you. Your integration won't save you.

Being able to talk openly about lesbian sex, openly declaring myself lesbian, states our existence, and demands entitlement to existence. As a political and social tactic, the openness declares that the best defense is a good offense. When we march down the streets shouting "never again," we are not naive enough to believe it couldn't happen again. The statement is also a warning: "Next time it's not going to be so easy for you to keep the closet door closed, humiliate us, kill us."

When I hear a non-lesbian define me by saying, "A lesbian is someone who likes making love to women," I want to respond by asking, "How? Do you know how?"

And I have to begin that answer by defining and examining my own excitement. There are few general statements which are absolutes for all lesbians. But I believe that this excitement is based on the natural eroticism inherent in sex between two women. The excitement comes precisely from the fact that it is two women and not a man and a woman.

The literature, art, film to which we have been exposed all of our lives states implicitly that heterosexual sex is exciting because there is the mystery of the other, the attraction of the opposites: a man and woman. We can refute this belief about heterosexual sex by focusing on the truth of our own sexual experiences.

The obvious reality of the biological similarities of our bodies is that rather than deadening sexual mystery, as we have been told, similarity is a powerful source of sexual excitement. These biological similarities are the basis, the core of the excitement implicit in the physiological identification.

For the sake of comparison with heterosexual sex, I will discuss only one aspect of lesbian sex — penetration with hands. This is only one example. It is not meant to represent all lesbian sex practices. It should not be interpreted as categorizing or defining lesbian sexual expression.

When I enter another woman with my hand, my fingers, I know what she feels like, physiologically. I may not know her emotional feelings, her reaction to me, but I do know her body. I may know what it feels like to have fingers inside of me. I recognize the inside of her body. It is my body. And

I know what she is feeling at that moment when my fingers enter her.

This moment of identification, communication and recognition of shared sensations is very complex. It is her body entered. It is my body entering. It is my body responding. My body responding to the feeling of my fingers entering her. My body responding to her feeling that same sensation. I identify with what she is physically experiencing at that moment. I can feel her in my fingers, in my head and inside me. She experiences the sensation inside her, and in her head. She, too, identifies with my feeling. She knows that I am experiencing the excitement of this moment and she knows, too, the way in which I experience it. It is not only my identification with her which causes the excitation, it is also her knowing what I am feeling and her identification with me.

I am conscious of this flow between two women. The awareness of the feelings and sensations is an integral part of the excitement. The flow is energy, power, discovery, recognition. My fingers inside of someone, I can also feel fingers inside of me. At this moment I am the receiver and the giver. I identify with the sensation of being entered and with the person performing the act. I know the feeling in my own body. My physical sensations intensify because of this psychological identification. The excitement comes both from her and from me.

Descriptions of this sexual moment appear in many lesbian works of fiction. I would like to quote from several novels to illustrate the universality of these feelings.

> ...her senses were filled with Megan. Her eyes closed as her fingers entered Megan. She was stunned by the soft warmth that encircled her. She moved instinctively, and

with each movement she felt Megan's body respond with pleasure. She was intoxicated by her own power. A power to move another human being to a state of obvious joy. To touch a woman and know the fire that had consumed her own body moments before now burned in this woman's soul. [7]

This awareness of the physiological similarities can intensify into a deeper spiritual sensation of connection, sometimes, a mystical union. One woman may feel that she is reaching up and touching the deepest part of another's being.

Jacqui gasped with pleasure as Lia's fingers entered her, first one, then another and finally, another. Three fingers filling her, stroking and thrusting, and again and again rubbing her clitoris, bringing her closer and closer to the point of no return. It felt as though Lia were holding the center of Jacqui's being in a single hand, caught between those strong, knowledgeable fingers, urging her on and on and on.[8]

During these moments of sexual identification and unity, it is possible for the woman entering to have an orgasm solely from the response of the woman being entered, and/or from her own identification with the sensations and the feeling of that other woman.

Carolyn's orgasms were like coming herself, and she could not feel the sensations enough. And Val understood that if she made Carolyn come a hundred times it would not extinguish her own fire.[9]

I don't think that a man can ever feel that identification. He has no idea what that woman is experiencing at that moment. I do. He cannot identify with that woman. No matter what the relationship, he will never be able to appreciate that moment when entry into another woman becomes entry into yourself.

No man can even imagine what making love feels like to the woman. He can only understand his own physical reactions and identify with the sensations that he is experiencing. A lesbian lover can concentrate on herself, understand and identify with the other woman, focus both on the feeling in her fingers and the feeling that the other woman is experiencing in her vagina.

In addition, the level of intimacy of the sexual partners may also increase the identification and heighten the excitation. But, the truth is, in lesbian sex it really doesn't matter how intimately you know another woman. You know her body. You know how another woman feels inside. It is your body, too. This communication can be sufficient stimulus for excitation.

> She felt Pat's fingers slide into her and rose to enclose them. She trembled when the fingers slowly withdrew in a long caress. Her hips lifted higher in trembling response.... She felt as if Pat were reaching into her depths toward a center of intensity, and she moved in rhythm to Pat's fingers, pulling inward.... When she reached into Pat, feeling the silky, warm wetness, hearing Pat's sharp intake of breath, her gratification was as great as when Pat had made love to her. She pulled herself up on one elbow and watched the younger woman succumb to her touch.[10]

This duality in lesbian sex can never exist in hetero-sex in the same way, because in heterosexual sex there can never be such a basic knowledge of the other's body. Nor can there be equality of the sexual act reflected in body similarity and societal situation.

The duality of lesbian sex affects the excitement. One woman knows that she may, either simultaneously or sequentially, experience similar sensations. This anticipation heightens the sexual responses. The awareness of becoming giver, or/and receiver, increases the identification with the sex partner.

This alternating "power" role is an important element in lesbian sex. I use the term "power" in a sexual context, as a created image playing out an aspect of sexuality. A lesbian can choose to be both players. Roles can be reversed. Each woman may get the chance to experience both parts of this sex play, in a unique way, different from hetero-sex. While being made love to, a woman can relax, give in, allow herself to assume the role of the one being entered. When entering, a woman realizes another part of her personality.

There are real difficulties in describing lesbian sex. As there is no name for lesbian relationships, there is no language appropriate for lesbian sex. Yet the language we do use can affect our sexual lives. As an example, imagine that the first woman is placing two or three fingers inside of the second woman, who is lying on her back with her legs open. This is purely descriptive. The first woman is doing this. The second woman is doing that. The broad description has no real overtones of connotation. Say, we then attempt to define further what these two women are doing: we say the first woman is the lover and the second woman is the lov-ee; the first woman is the giver, the second woman is the receiver; the first woman is the top, the second woman is the bottom;

that additional language transforms the action. It seems as if the second woman is now passive. She is the receiver of the action. The language does not express the simultaneity of feeling in both women. Nor does it convey the mutual participation in this act. The descriptions detract from the reality of lesbian sex reducing one person to "performer" and the other to the "performed upon." This does not describe lesbian sex at all.

Using these words may have an effect on lesbian sex partners. They may respond to the roles assigned by language definition. Lesbians may not live in the reality of the act itself, not recognize the inadequacies of the language, but react to and be affected by definitions of a language which does not really describe them or what they are feeling or doing. Calling ourselves, lover-lov-ee, top-bottom, giver-receiver will not do. The word "lovers" implies too much emotion to describe a physical act. The words "giver" and "receiver" send the wrong message, implying that one is either passive or active. Language denies the essence of lesbian sex: the simultaneity of feeling and the mutuality of physical identity.

As a lesbian, I must be conscious of who I am. There are no single, simple answers to questions raised in discussing lesbian sex. In fact, the more discussions, the more questions seem to arise. And this is how it should be.

In writing this paper, I thought about us as the group that Jill Johnston once described as the Lesbian Nation.[11] The diversity of our sexual needs and desires should not make talking about our sexuality impossible. We are not all the same. Nor should people who comprise a nation be thought of as similar. The need to re-think old ideas is vital to our future lesbian lives. Our differences and similarities should encourage us to re-create and define our selves in a truer, more realistic, positive and energetic way.

Endnotes

1. Lyndall MacCowan, "Recollecting history, renaming lives: Femme stigma and the feminist seventies and eighties," in *The Persistent Desire: A Femme-Butch Reader,* ed. Joan Nestle (Boston: Alyson Publications, 1992), 322.
2. Carole Vance, "Gender Systems, Ideology and Sex Research," in *Powers of Desire, The Politics of Sexuality,* ed. Ann Snitow, Christine Stansell, and Sharon Thompson (New York: Monthly Review Press, 1983), 375-376.
3. Monique Wittig, *The Straight Mind* (Boston: Beacon Press, 1992), 4.
4. Ibid., 32.
5. Julia Penelope, *Call Me Lesbian* (California: Crossing Press, 1992), 42.
6. I am speaking only of lesbian sex and make no assumptions about gay male sex.
7. Evelyn Kennedy, *Cherished Love* (Tallahassee, Florida: Naiad Press, 1988), 59.
8. H. H. Johanna, *Romancing the Dream* (New York: Rising Tide Press, 1991), 71.
9. Katherine V. Forrest, *An Emergence of Green* (Tallahassee, Florida: Naiad Press, 1986), 183.
10. Jackie Calhoun, *Lifestyles* (Tallahassee, Florida: Naiad Press, 1990), 169-170.
11. Jill Johnston, *Lesbian Nation* (Random House, 1973).

In a Complex Weave

Sheila
Batacharya

Coming Out

My coming out involved more than reviving and accepting myself as a lesbian. I feel that every time I have uncovered pain or memory I go through a coming-out process. For this reason I sometimes find the gay and lesbian community alienating. How do I talk about coming out just as a lesbian when my experiences of racism, classism and sexism have had such a huge impact on the decisions I have made and the identities I embody? I was not always aware that being labeled a paki, a bitch or poor was connected to a bigger picture. Coming out, for me, means dropping the shame that I've carried with me for most of my life, about all of who I am.

When a mixed-race women's group was formed in Toronto, I reluctantly made a commitment to myself to attend the first meeting. This was shortly after I had come out as a lesbian, a process of claiming a sexuality that was new in some respects while at the same time very familiar. When I returned home that night I was overwhelmed with painful memories and a sense of profound loneliness. The issues that had been raised by myself and the other women attending the meeting made me feel that there was something unavoidably problematic about being mixed race. I felt somewhat comforted in the presence of other mixed-race women, thankfully many of whom were lesbians and bisexual women. But at the same time I felt that I did not want to be who I was, and I have to move through, what was for me, uncharted territory.

Racism and Homophobia — Each Experience Shaping the Other

My experience and identity are not limited to, and solely constructed through, race. I feel the core of my awareness, through which I have understood the intersection of systemic oppressions, has been shaped by my experience of sexism, homophobia and classism, as well as racism. I cannot isolate one aspect of my reality because each experience effects the others. With respect to my experiences as a mixed-race woman, my analysis has involved examining how privilege as well as alienation has figured in my experience of racism.

My mother is Canadian born, of Irish and French heritage; my father is from Calcutta, India. I have lived in Canada all my life. Although there may be similarities, my experience will be different from someone who is mixed race and has two parents of colour. Living in Canada, growing up as a child of an immigrant to Canada, is also a factor in my experiences and analysis. I believe that I come from a relatively privileged position as a mixed-race person. Colonized people living in their homeland or enslaved people displaced and kidnapped have a history, which may result in an analysis of being mixed race that stems from a point of reference involving experiences different from mine. It has never been my goal or intention to seek out the definitive analysis of mixed-race identity. Such a notion is in itself contrary to my experience as a mixed-race woman.

My awareness of racism developed before I came out as a dyke. It was while working in the feminist community for the first time that my analysis and consciousness of race and class oppression exploded. I was furious at the lack of space and energy allocated to addressing these issues and at the expectation that race and class, as oppressions, were secondary to gender. In a predominantly white middle-class environment it was easier to be clear about my experience of race and class. This is when I "came out" as a woman of colour and started to deal with my own internalized racism.

One of the first times I thought about where my experience of racism as a mixed-race woman located me was when I replied to an ad at the university for a room for rent which was available to women of colour who were either lesbian or lesbian positive. I knew that I wanted to live with dykes, but I felt apprehensive identifying myself as a woman of colour to another South Asian woman. I remember questioning myself "if I counted," because *only* my father was Indian. After years of dreading queries such as "Where are you from?" or "What are you?" I found it unfamiliar to acknowledge, in a positive way, my South Asian heritage.

As I started to identify as a woman of colour in the white feminist community, I felt quite secure about how my experience of racism had affected me. I looked at my white childhood friends and my only extended family — my mother's family — and the source of much of the pain and anger I had experienced presented itself. Similarly, when I came out as a lesbian I knew who I was in relation to whom I had been told to be. In coming out as a dyke I was confused but I also felt strong. As I directed my energies to working in solidarity with women of colour I began to consider my experience as a woman of South Asian descent. I was confronted with my lack of community. I had spent my childhood and adolescence chasing a white identity; the identity I was most exposed to outside the contact with my father. This is when I began a sort of coming-out process as a mixed-race woman of colour. The difficulty was that I didn't know what to do with my experience as a mixed-race woman. There is no politic for me as a mixed-race woman that is separate from my identity as a woman of colour. As a lesbian, at times, I could at least find solace — politically and emotionally — in my identity as a dyke. I felt just the opposite when I thought about my experiences as a mixed-race woman.

Overlapping Communities/Identities

Through the construction of identity within white supremacy I feel that I do not fit into the dichotomy of white people vs. people of colour. In white culture my identity as a woman of colour is erased. In a South Asian context my existence is traced to colonization. Racism precludes both of these realities.

I remember clearly as a child that I felt that I was an experiment, an abberation of nature. I knew that I was not white; however, feeling apart from white culture was something I tried not to think about. I tried not to question the absence of a sense of community in my life. In adulthood, as I became exposed to community-based anti-racist activism and identity politics, I started to realize the ways in which being mixed race impacted on my sense of identity. When I thought about the fact that I did not grow up feeling as part of a community based on race and culture I felt isolated as well as robbed. Occasionally, I still feel this way, but now I think of community as something one builds for themselves and for others. It is by no means a monolithic-contained grouping. Each community I identify with seems to be a joining of many communities together. I feel very grateful that there are communities of men and women who celebrate and build upon this complexity by coming together and making alliances that challenge not only one form of oppression but also work towards fighting all forms of injustice and discrimination.

Talking about mixed race issues is one way I have come to understand that racism is a construction. As a mixed-race woman, it has been a long journey to the realization that, whatever stereotypes and assumptions people have about who I must be, these have less to do with who I am than with stereotypes constructed through white supremacy and patriarchy. With this in mind I have worked with the Canadian feminist movement as well as with the South Asian and the lesbian of colour communities. In meeting with mixed-race women of many different ancestries, I have felt empowered and supported by sharing our thoughts and experiences. Just to know that there are other mixed-race women, and more specifically lesbians, who sometimes experience the world in similar ways, is extremely comforting.

Privilege/Power

Sorting through and identifying issues of privilege, power and oppression is complicated. I have never been able to use a single-issue pyramid like structure of oppression to conceptualize what I have seen or experienced. In my parents' relationship, I witnessed my father's experience of racism in his marriage to my mother as well as in the Canadian society. I was also aware of his privilege as a man which, at times, he abused. My mother, who comes from a working-class white background, experienced sexism and misogyny in her marriage and as a psychiatric survivor. Discrimination of people with mental illness is an issue that has had also a huge impact on the way I view society. Putting into context my father's experience of racism, his privilege as a man, my mother's experience of misogyny and her privilege as a white woman, has made me aware of the need to understand how oppressions, as well as privilege, intersect and how these affect interactions between people. Critically examining this has been an important step to understanding and working in solidarity with those who struggle against multiple oppressions. It has also been the reason I feel it is important to always identify and be responsible about one's own power and to be aware of one's ability to abuse power depending on the situation. My mother and father come from different places of pain and discrimination. What has been very hard to witness is the lack of respect for each other's experiences and to see how disempowered people use what privilege they may have to lash out at one another, striking where each is most vulnerable.

I can now identify that when my family received bomb threats it was racist violence, while at the same time I see that going to the Canadian National Exhibition with white folks (family) meant that my dad, sister and I were not as easily targeted. We did not experience racism in the same way people of colour would, who were not in the presence of, and in many ways, under the protection of white friends or relatives. Examining the advantages of having a white family and light skin and validating my experiences of racism within my mother's family and in the Canadian society have been ways through which I have been able to develop clarity around my identity. Freeing up the energy previously spent on the confusion and pain of sorting through identity politics as a mixed-race dyke has made it easier to put my energy where I want it to be: working in anti-oppression movements.

Living with many different power dynamics helped me realize that intricate manifestations of oppression and internalized racism, sexism, classism and homophobia exist. Being mixed race is only one aspect of my being, through which I developed a consciousness around the abuse of power and the links between different oppressions. Coming out as a lesbian has also been an integral part of developing this consciousness. I cannot separate racism from sexism and/or heterosexism in, for example, my experiences of being exotified as a mixed-race woman or a lesbian of colour by either men or women, straight or queer. In a complex weave, racism, heterosexism, sexism and classism figure in the way each oppression impacts upon me. None of these experiences can be sifted or sorted out from the whole of my life. I used to find this confusing but now I just think it's complex.

Queer across Canada:
A Videographer's Journey

Maureen
Bradley

DECEMBER 1991: a friend shows me a piece of paper that will alter my life: an application for something called "Road Movies," a CBC series that will send eight young videographers across the country to videotape "their vision of Canada." Compelling, I thought, but if they saw *my* vision of Canada they'd probably go into convulsions. At the age of twenty-four, I was a self-identified loud-mouthed dyke, I firmly believed that it was essential for me to be out as a dyke in all aspects of my life — whenever possible.

I wasn't sure if the people who drafted the application could stomach my vision of Canada. While I fully believed that I should have the right to stand among the ranks of the chosen few and tell my stories, I knew that the CBC often forgets that its mandate is to reflect the multiplicity of Canadian "identity" and consciousness back to Canadian public.[1] (A certain queer 10 per cent rarely, if ever, grace our TV screens.) I doubted if they would, in fact, want to see my vision of Canada. But, I remembered that the CBC had done some progressive and experimental programming ("Pilot One," "Kids in the Hall," "Degrassi Talks") and kept that in mind while writing my application. I knew I was the right person for the job, but did they?

With all that in mind, I was "out" in my application and my interviews, but not blatantly so. I couldn't help being out since much of my work involved lesbian and gay communities. It was clear in my mind that my vision of Canada would obviously be mediated through my lesbian identity and subjectivity. In the application they asked us to describe who we were — so I did. There was never any question about being in or out. They wanted to know who I was, I told them. In my application I described myself as a shit-disturber and crossed my fingers figuring that if there were women involved in the production they, too, would have to be shit-disturbers to get where they are.[2]

APRIL 1992: To my surprise I was selected to be one of eight young "ambassadors of the CBC" for the summer and fall of 1992. My roommate was sure it was a joke, that they would eventually call me back and say "Sorry, we made a mistake, we can't put a lesbian on national television."

When I left Montréal for training I felt unsure, terrified, excited, but most of all, I felt like a spy infiltrating the great unknown enemy — mainstream media. I was to be the first lesbian, to my knowledge, allowed to be out on a Canadian national television series as something other than a news story or a pathetically depressed or chronically bisexual character on a drama series. But surprisingly there was no fanfare, no massive headline in the *Globe and Mail*. It seemed to me that this was historic, but precisely because it was historic, I knew it wouldn't be easy. I knew I would have to be more clever and cunning than my straight counterparts if I was to get my "vision of Canada" aired on prime-time TV.

When I got to the training session I discovered I was not alone. There was another dyke on the show who, coincidentally, had also described herself as a shit disturber in her application. She would become my only true ally for months down the road — the only one who would fully understand the painful ubiquitousness of systemic heterosexism and how it can manifest itself in such a "progressive" show, the only one who could share the pain and difficulty of trying to confront this heterosexism.

SUMMER 1993: I see a call for submissions for an anthology of combatting heterosexism and homophobia and wonder if I can take all these raw emotions I felt during "Road Movies" and actually make sense of them to document my most difficult experience resisting heterosexism. I sat down shortly after the whole experience and wrote everything that came to mind about the "Road Movies" experience, a twenty-page stream-of-consciousness rant that helped me exorcise my demons. But I wonder now if it's worth submitting, it seems so incredibly self-evident to me. But that is the point: it is self-evident, and yet I've never read anything that describes this incredibly common experience. On the road, my main problem was that I had no guidance. That resulted in an immense feeling of isolation. I knew countless other gays and lesbians had experienced what I was going through, but I couldn't find their words anywhere. The purpose of revising this rant/manuscript, would be to try and start documenting those self-evident struggles.

I want other lesbians, gay men and bisexuals who combat resistance when coming out publicly to know that they're not the only ones. There are certain patterns and cycles that seem to recur when so-called marginalized people start taking up space in society, certain cycles of resentment from others and anger in oneself that often, if not always, seem to occur. These cycles are merely a subtler layer of systemic discrimination and they serve, or at the very least, attempt to roll back some of the freedoms we have achieved. Now that I have the critical distance to put these patterns into perspective, what strikes me the most is how the expression of homophobia and heterosexism is quite unimaginative and just plain boring. But, I felt like I was on uncharted territory, even though I knew I wasn't. When we share the stories and strategies of our struggle, the same boring patterns crop up again and again. When we know this, half the struggle is over. Therefore, it is imperative that we start sharing these self-evident stories. This is what I've tried to document here.

SUMMER 1992: The poster for the series looks like a Benetton ad, or so I've been told. The press release touted the sexual, racial and regional diversity of the group — four men, four women, two women of colour, one Native man, a New-foundlander, a Québécois man and two lesbians, though our lesbianism was never announced with fanfare in the press release the way the other signifiers of diversity were. We may have looked like a Benetton ad, or an affirmative-action commercial, but the producers soon found out we acted like neither. Though the group may have possessed the surface marks of diverse identities, our individual senses of identity were anything but superficial. Some of the videographers identified strongly along regional, racial or sexual trajectories and were interested in "Road Movies" precisely because they wanted our visions represented in the mainstream. We were confident that our stories were valid and knew it was time they were finally heard. This attitude, I was later told repeatedly, amounted to an "agenda," when not expressed subtly enough. "'Road Movies' was never intended to be anyone's soapbox" was a refrain I also heard a number of times during the seven months of production. The very real difference in the social conditions of some of the videographers and the CBC execs created the gap in perception labeled as soapbox. Their soapbox was my reality.

Many of the problems that arose with "Road Movies" may have resulted because the show was one big experiment for all those involved. The network was apparently very nervous about the show. It was the first time they aired a series without having first produced a pilot episode. Furthermore they were relying on eight completely unknown "kids" to produce quality prime-time TV for six months straight. In their terms, they *were* taking a big risk. The producers had a certain vision of the show, but were more tightly controlled by the network than they expected to be. When we went into production, much of what they had taught us in training was immediately abandoned because of the incredible financial constraints and also because the network probably got scared.

The premise of the show was to have eight young people constantly moving through different parts of the country as a one- person crew to find and collect different stories that would air weekly. We would work alone and be responsible for all aspects of shooting the story, finding it, researching it, interviewing, shooting, doing the sound, narration, writing, doing on-camera intros. We were also responsible for doing a paper-edit for each piece; we would then send our tapes by couriers to Ottawa where they would edit each piece and produce the show. We were told that we had complete artistic control over our pieces and the production team would only intervene to clean up technical problems.

The show and its promos led the audience to believe that this was in fact what they were watching, our unmediated "vision of Canada."

After a few weeks on the road it became clear to me that I had very little control over how my character was being mediated. Much of what I shot was altered in the editing process. Many times it was for the better (since all the videographers were young and had no experience in broadcasting), but when a delicate political issue was involved, chances are the piece would somehow be altered from the original version. In the end we did *not* have control over our stories,[3] and in a sense I felt I was being misrepresented. This is where the real power struggle happened. And this is where I found a lot of misunderstandings arose between myself and the production team because of the subtle and not-so-subtle influence of heterosexism on the production process.

Because everything was an experiment, there were no rules. This created a bizarre and unstable working environment. I was never exactly sure what my role was as a videographer. When we were in Toronto for training, I thought we would act mainly as documentary makers who would subtly situate or position themselves within the text. We were later told to emphasize more our *point of view* in each story. During a shoot for the show's promo, a makeup artist told us that we were going to become *commodities,* a declaration that made many of us gag. Towards the end of the show — most of the pieces were very strongly character-driven — we were told halfway through the production process that we needed to be "characters" the audience identified with and wanted to follow each week. I was never sure exactly what my job was because it kept shifting.

It took an immense amount of energy to continually try

to educate those involved with the production about my identity. As videographers we held very little, if not the least amount of power, in the whole process. That burden was so hard to describe to my straight producers that it very often left me angry, tired, in tears, wanting to give up, asking myself how I ever wound up in the bizarre role of attempting to educate the "mainstream," something I had never particularly been interested in before. It seemed to me that the struggle for the other lesbian on the show, however, was much harder. Being a woman of colour and a lesbian, she seemed constantly frustrated with and confined by the limitations of the show's discourse. Since I came out on the show towards the beginning of the series, it seemed somehow that she was not permitted to do so, though it was never stated as such. All her queer stories somehow got re-edited at mission control to omit references towards her sexuality. As such, I believe she experienced an even harder burden of having her sexuality continually erased and denied.

Furthermore, the show was partially sponsored by Canada 125,[4] which made me cringe. I felt completely at odds with what I was doing. On the one hand, I felt the show was selling out on a political level, yet I recognized the importance of my visibility as a lesbian on a national TV show for twenty-six weeks.

JUNE 20, 1992: *Edmonton, Pride Week. I'm amazed at how organized the community is here. This afternoon while riding on a high, meeting great people and having a great time — BANG — I read a local prairie gay publication and see an article about a project on lesbians and gays in Canada that was rejected by Canada 125 — our major sponsor. The Canada 125 guy quoted in the article is being openly homophobic: "I don't have to tell you this is a controversial issue* *(gays and lesbians); we can't risk it because we have corporate funding."* Do they realize that their flagship project involves two big dykes? I'm in a rage — but what can I do sitting alone in my barren room at the YWCA? I want to fly directly to Toronto and chain myself to the Canada 125 office, then call in the news crew. But what can I really do — can I make any kind of positive change within this system? How can I be involved in this? Maybe I should just quit now before I lose my mind.*

JULY 21, 1992: *Yellowknife, in a hotel I'm not paying for, I'm watching the fourth episode of "Road Movies." Well I've just come out on national TV. I was kind of nervous watching it but it was really anti-climactic. The piece was a minute and a half long and it just showed us all having fun at gay pride day in Toronto — 100,000 people attended. I can't believe they aired it!!!???? I did it — I got it on and it wasn't even hard — and it's only the fourth show! But then again it was really inoffensive, it was a really bland story in my mind but it's probably as far as they're able to go. Maybe it won't be as bland for queers in rural Alberta to see 100,000 happy, visible gays and lesbians taking over downtown Toronto. Funny. There were also 100,000 people at Canada 125's Canada Day celebrations in Ottawa, but they wouldn't let me say that on TV. Oh, well, I guess it's better than nothing. I wonder if that homophobic executive at Canada 125 saw it.*

The sheer fact of our representation on "Road Movies" changes the whole arena of meaning for Canada 125, the notion of "Canadianness" portrayed on the show, and the CBC's policy commitment towards fostering a "shared national consciousness and identity"[5] for Canada. Different segments of the show were buffered by a continual barrage of Canada 125 commercials and Multiculturalism and Citizenship Canada commercials — all showing a happy, smiling, diverse Canada that only exists in policy and not in practice. Some of the show's segments were an odd contrast to these nauseating commercials showing an artificial and imagined unity and community. The show sometimes dealt with racism, single moms, life on Native reserves, male and female sex trade workers, gays and lesbians of many colours, an abortion clinic and a host of other brief moments of televisual disruption. These items disrupted the grand narrative of national unity and identity and the Canada 125 hoopla that began to look farcical during many of the commercial breaks. On the other hand, there were a number of feel-good, typically Canadian stories about the land, fishing, hunting, tourism, the railway, the army and all sorts of other signifiers of an unquestioned "Canadianness." The moments of rupture, though few, were sweet, and they pushed the limits of what the CBC will air under the aegis of youth-entertainment programming.

Many of the videographers knew that we did not see ourselves reflected on Canadian TV as we were growing up, even though the mandate of the CBC is, as I've already stated, among other things, to reflect Canada back to Canadians. In my mind, it was only logical that we finally got to do it. But it wasn't easy. There was resistance on the part of the "corp" and some of its high-powered executives. A policy for diversity is simple enough (which the 1991 Broadcasting Act has enshrined), but actually trying to put those intentions into practice rustled up notions of reverse discrimination, self-indulgence, lack of balance, lack of objectivity and the touting of various agendas. Only the videographers were charged with having agendas, the corporation and production crew were assumed to be immune from such things. It is clear to me that everyone has a bias or, to use a nastier term, agenda. In my experience, when certain individuals are aware of their bias and are upfront about it, they're called radicals or characterized as activists or members of "special interest groups." Yet those who aren't aware of their bias are characterized as just people or average citizens. It was strange to come from a feminist milieu, where the proper thing to do is to put your point of view, bias or privilege, on the table. In the new CBC milieu, I was confronted with the assumption that all "normal" people are objective, fair and usually level-headed, no agendas are present.

There was an intangible notion of an "audience" that dictated controversial content decisions based on assumptions about what material that "audience" might possibly disapprove of. This notion of audience kept the show appearing polite and innocent throughout most of its air time. The perceived values and tastes of a fictitious norm always overrode a piece that might speak to or validate the experiences of a certain minority viewership and, maybe, even in the process enlighten or, dare I say it, entertain, the fictitious norm. It is perhaps this invisible imagined audience of "normal" Canadians that is responsible for keeping the CBC, as a government-sponsored cultural industry, a little too bland.[6]

Many viewers whom I encountered on the road told me that judging from the show's slick promo, they thought the show would be a lot more cutting edge, a lot more experimental and a lot more real. Conversely, many viewers thought it *was* a lot more "real" than say, "Degrassi High," but I think many of the videographers and production team expected the show to be much more than it was. We were told in training to "break the rules" but when our tapes started being edited, the rules became a lot more inflexible. The ever-powerful imagined audience was invoked when stories seemed a bit too risky. The queer part of the audience was never imaginable; I was never allowed to speak directly to them, because the rest of the audience would apparently be offended. "Why preach to the converted?" I was told. I was never allowed to display any anger in relation to homophobia, racism or anything, it seemed, because "anger is alienating to the mainstream audience." Funny, I spent many hours in front of the TV as a woman and as a lesbian being alienated by mainstream television, but somehow that was not relevant any more. The all-pervasive invisible audience always overruled.

SPRING 1993: The cover of *New York* magazine shows a pouting kd lang with a bold proclamation to her left in white, italic, feminine typeface "The New Lesbian Chic." A month latter, *Newsweek* also has lesbians on the cover. We have finally been discovered by the American mainstream media! Many dykes I talk to think it's great — it's a real example of our progress and how society has become more tolerant. But these magazine covers scare me more than they excite me. Now that mainstream media is covering lesbianism it can also attempt to "define" what (acceptable) lesbianism is.

Gays and lesbians have been gaining in the area of mainstream representation over the past few years, so, in a sense, it wasn't a huge surprise to me that two lesbians would be selected to be on this "hip" new show. The problem arose when we wouldn't follow the subtle pleas to fit in. I wouldn't be a "designer dykes" or polite "gay women." I brought my radical activist politics with me and wouldn't settle for assimilation into a heterosexist norm. If I had been a nice gay woman like Sandra Bernhardt's character on "Roseanne," then everything would most likely have been fine, but I was unapologetically queer, part of a new generation queer agitators, not gay assimilationists.

I felt I was pushing the limits of the envelope constantly, and that was exhausting and frustrating. It seems we are embraced as part of the diversity of Canada as long as we behave. This is the problem I've encountered in non-queer or non-progressive environments, whether it's the CBC or elsewhere. You can be a dyke (or rather a gay woman) as long as you don't act like one, and whatever you do, don't make people uncomfortable by talking about homophobia and heterosexism all the time. In many liberal milieus I have worked in, including the CBC, it seemed people were into "diversity" and "equity" as long as the subjects of diversity act like white straight men. When they/we don't, look out.

The cycle of heterosexism is reinforced by omission. Many people I dealt with during the "Road Movies" experience thought I was out of control, pushing this "gay thing" too far and thus, perhaps, they felt justified in their continual heterosexism. Because you so rarely see any gay images on TV (except sensationalistic or negative ones), *any* image of lesbianism seems like it's too much. This lack of images is detrimental to everyone. Gays and lesbians need to see reflections of themselves to create positive self-esteem in a hateful society. Straight people have to start realizing that we exist. But this cycle, as I learnt last year, is difficult to break.

I think the simple visibility of some "Road Movies" videographers accomplished more than I, buried in the production process, realized. When viewers would approach me and thank me for coming out on TV, because their parents or friends had been watching, or when I received mail from young gays and lesbians living in small towns who said they were so glad to find out they weren't the only ones — it was only then that I realized the struggle to be out was worth it. In the end we were able to get a lot of controversial stuff on TV, stuff that was "our vision of Canada," questions and opinions that real young people have today. Some videographers fought to get something "controversial" aired. Each fight to get our "vision of Canada" on TV was exhausting. But we managed to provide the audience[7] with glimpses of young people rarely, if ever, seen on TV. That is all I wanted to do in the first place and though it wasn't easy, it did finally happen.

NOVEMBER 7, 1992: I am asked to speak to a group of student journalist at the Canadian University Press Western Regional Conference about being openly gay on national TV. Most of the participants want to talk about censorship — was I censored? I can't give a clear answer to the question. I was working within a large institutional bureaucracy, and like any other, there is systemic discrimination. The process of production and post-production involves so many people that it is impossible to say that any one force is suppressing someone's voice. Whenever pieces that I shot of a progressive political nature were rejected, there were always a number of technical or stylistic reasons offered as motivation for their rejection.

The hegemonic process and the "imagined majority audience" structured the process. Knowing that didn't make the negotiation through heterosexism any easier, it just gave me nowhere to focus my anger. I was fighting a fight only myself and the other lesbian on the show knew existed. I was fighting rules that my straight counterparts were most likely not aware of and probably didn't have to bother with. I often censored myself, as I'm sure the story producers also did. The imaginary audience and its assumed threshold of tolerance kept us in line more than any one great evil homophobic censor. This often frustrated me, it was hard to focus my energies on what blocked me. I was constantly second-guessing my work, censoring myself and questioning my whole complicity in a project endorsed by Canada 125.

But what was clear in all my discussions with the producers regarding the limits of acceptability was, that although the concept of audience guided many editorial decisions, the gay audience was never a priority *or even a reality.* Most of the CBC execs probably tried to imagine it out of existence. Nobody understood how large and loyal the gay audience is. What the fictitious majority could handle would always override the gay viewership. That straight viewers might actually be interested in seeing a gay perspective was never considered. I always thought they had the best focus group possible right in front of them — the eight videographers — but there was never a connection made between those behind the scenes and the imagined viewership. The videographers and production staff are *part* of the general public and mainstream audience. This link was never made and the all-pervasive intangible audience stayed intact.

While working on "Road Movies," I was called dogmatic, too politically correct, unsubtle and a host of other things. I think most of my critics aren't aware that many young people today *are* dogmatic and idealistic. The twentysomething generation is always defined by the media as apathetic and materialistic, going nowhere. My friends certainly don't fit that bill. Many young people today *are* angry.

Mainstream media tries to make us believe that anger and the expression of anger don't really exist in the mythical "mainstream" normal society. Anger is just a phenomenon of the radical fringe, real people don't react like that. Though I was never censored, I was told that my on-camera sequences couldn't be angry. The ones that were deemed too hostile were rejected or redone because, I was told, the tone would alienate the "audience." I was often angry about a lot of things I encountered on the road, but I had to streamline to the imagined audience. This erases the existence of anger as something that motivates a lot of Canadians.

NOVEMBER 15, 1992: *Somewhere in southern Ontario. One day when all this is finally all over I will make a conceptual art video where all I do for fifteen solid minutes is say the word "lesbian."*

LATE NOVEMBER 1992: The production stage of "Road Movies" will be over in a matter of weeks. I've managed to sneak away to "La Ville en Rose," a Québec conference on lesbian and gay studies. I feel human again surrounded by queers. However, I'm finding this conference, and the "Outrights" conference held in Vancouver in October, very frustrating. Both conferences are intended to cover a gamut of gay concerns. Nobody seems to be talking about the dilemma I have been living in for six months — systemic heterosexism. Now, granted it's not as fun as discussing lesbian pulp novels or "Basic Instinct," but I imagine it as something my peers and elders have a considerable amount of experience with. I know I am not the only one navigating the treacherous course through blatant heterosexism. I wonder if other people who have experienced being out in mainstream institutions can validate my experience. I ask a number of speakers questions about their strategies for dealing with heterosexism in the mainstream, but nobody seems to find this topic terribly exciting. Desire and identity have a lot more currency in queer theory today, but I'm telling whoever will listen — we don't live in a vacuum.

JUNE 1993: Younger gays and lesbians who have come out in a seemingly more tolerant environment than existed 20 years ago need practical advice on how to navigate our way through the straight world. Tolerance is superficial. Tolerance is also conditional, as I've said above. There are reactions and patterns I encountered during "Road Movies" and in other straight environments where I have been out. Once you come out, many straight people view your life as an *issue* — not as a life in all its complexity. Though you show them much more, they perceive only one aspect of your life . Some label you as repressive or too politically correct if you simply talk about being a lesbian, though they never shut up about their heterosexuality. Many will charge you with "flaunting it" simply by being out, even though heterosexuality is forced down our throats everywhere in popular culture. Often this leads people to judge you as being "biased" and this can result in a perceived "loss of objectivity." This was a crucial pattern in my case; I was seen to be less objective than my straight male counterparts. By standing up for one part of my identity, I seemed to lose all other parts of my identity. This often happens the minute one states an interest in feminism, anti-racism, gay rights or even the environment. In broadcasting or journalism, this can have a debilitating career effect: you lose your "objectivity" while those around, especially straight white men, keep their objectivity intact. Oddly enough, I have met few straight people who were aware that their sexuality made *them* biased. Few heterosexuals are aware of their straight privilege. So many people I've worked with still ask me, "But what does it matter who you sleep with — we're all equal?" When will they finally figure out that it matters whom I sleep with because it matters whom "they" sleep with.

When the cycle of heterosexism is pushed to its limit, you will be expected to *prove* that you face discrimination. What you say won't be taken at face value unless you can prove it. Proof has lots of currency in the media. Queers are infinitely more interesting when they're bashed, pathetic or dying. This keeps the hierarchy of hetero/homo intact, by questioning and sensationalizing gay and lesbian experience against a heterosexual norm.

DECEMBER 1992: The show is finally over. I feel like I'm *sick* of being a lesbian. For seven months I was treated, talked to and talked about as a person with a unitary identity! I'm sick of talking about it, pointing it out, explaining it. Many of the people I worked with thought I was only interested in "gay stories" although I only shot four "gay stories" out of about sixty-five pieces in all. My reaction isn't because that's all I talk about — but for many people, it's all *they* hear, and sometimes it's all they are willing or able to perceive. Something has left this feeling with me, it's not something I've imagined. It's a very real effect of systemic heterosexism and it has left a scar on me.

JANUARY 1993: Now that I have some distance from this experience I've been able to get over the initial anger and gain some perspective. I've had to separate the personal effects of heterosexism from the real gains and growths I experienced. I would be the first to admit that the experience was also incredibly positive. Given the choice, I would do it again in a second. I met some remarkable people on my journeys and was taken in and supported by a network of women and lesbian communities across the country. Seeing queer communities across the country I also developed a commitment to staying in Canada and fostering queer culture here. We experience American cultural imperialism through the expression and articulation of our lesbian and gay identities just as much as we experience American cultural imperialism through our media and entertainment networks. The experience gave me a desire to make things happen in this country. It was also incredibly rewarding to see my producers react, adjust and learn from the challenges myself and the other videographers presented them with. I walked away from the experience knowing that these women, who wield a certain amount of power in the media community and for whom I have the utmost respect, now have a greater understanding of some of the realities that young dykes face. Their definition of lesbian undoubtedly shifted.

JULY 1993: If I've achieved nothing more than simple visibility of "lesbianism" on "Road Movies," that in itself is a revolutionary act. If that kind of momentary visibility makes it easier for some kids out there to sift through the bullshit and figure out who they are, then I couldn't be more pleased. Every time one of us comes out publicly, proclaims that we're here, we're queer, that we're proud, that we're happy, that we will take up space, that we will demand the same rights and privileges that hets have *always* taken for granted, every time we stand our ground with confidence, it makes it that much easier for the next person, it pushes the ebb of social change to a point where we can never go back to the old ways of blatant, and sometimes subtle, heterosexism.

Endnotes

1. *Canadian Broadcasting Act, 1991*, section 3(1)(m).

2. This was the case. The executive producer was a feminist running her own production company.

3. Towards the end of the show I was rudely told that I should just get used to not having any control over my work — "that's what the industry is like, kid." I know now that very few people involved in broadcasting do get any control over how they are mediated. But we were led to believe differently and, as optimistic and naive young people, some of us believed it. As the show developed and the videographers became "characters," it was clear that we were blurring the lines between fact and fiction — which is what most good TV does, even the news. We were relying on *codes* of realism, and not actual "reality," that heightened viewing pleasure but were quite far removed from "reality." Our characters became personas — hence, the feeling of misrepresentation. I realize, in retrospect, that I wasn't particularly misrepresented, but merely sucked into the television apparatus.

4. Canada 125 was the official organization responsible for celebrating Canada's 125th birthday. A fifth of their multimillion-dollar budget came from taxpayers and the rest was matched by corporate sponsors. The organization took applications for different community events from across the country.

   They refused to sponsor one very apolitical project called "A Family Portrait," which deals with gays and lesbians in Canada. Later, many of the same people from "A Family Portrait" reapplied with an almost identical project that was for owners of toy poodles, instead of gays and lesbians. The toy-poodle project was approved by Canada 125 and given sponsorship. When the story hit the press, there was a minor embarrassing scandal for Canada 125. This incident occurred well after I hit the road, but I was leery of Canada 125 from the beginning. They were a state-sanctioned unity vehicle and "Road Movies" could be viewed as nothing more than a nationalist platform that coincided quite nicely with the Charlottetown Accord.

   I found the whole idea of celebration quite problematic,

including Montreal's 350th anniversary, which I was fortunate enough to miss, and the 500th anniversary celebration of Columbus' arrival in the Americas. I did two pieces that dealt with 500 years of resistance; neither aired on the show.

5. *Canadian Broadcasting Act, 1991*, section 3(1)(m)(vi).

6. Of course, the rebuttal to such claims for fair proportional representation would be that people in our society just aren't ready to handle it yet, and that the CBC as government-funded cultural institution would come under fire from conservative back-benchers.

   I find it odd that Britain, a country many North Americans view as much more prudish and uptight about sexuality than we are, has had access to a weekly prime-time program on Channel 4 called "Out on Tuesday" that deals specifically with issues that concern gays and lesbians. "Out on Tuesday" has been on the air for a number of years and produces "quality" programming that has received critical acclaim at film festivals around the world. The Canadian version of "Sesame Street" recently started running segments on same-sex parents to catch up with the reality that young people face today. Perhaps, one day, prime-time TV in Canada will catch up with the cutting edge of children's programming.

7. The viewership was approximately half a million for the first thirteen episodes and about 350,000 for the last thirteen episodes. It covered all age groups proportionally and the accumulated audience for the entire series was 10 million.

Sensuous Being and the Role of Homophobia

Connie Fife

Thoughts whirl around in my head, twist themselves into some kind of shape. I play with a word and taste its meaning in the pit of my stomach: "homophobia." The word just won't stand still. It leaps around, performing its deformed dance, enticing me to follow its rhythm. I am obsessed with this word, so I follow. I dance to a dictionary where "homo" — a word I have heard time and again, rolls off my tongue, means, same, equal, like. "Phobia," *Webster* tells me, means persistent, insane dread or fear. Bring the two together and "homophobia" emerges.

Fear of sexuality begins inside and is related to what lies inside. I dive back into the dictionary and find that this word, "homophobia," does not exist. It is not defined. The fear of sameness and equality is housed within our own ribcages. Interesting that *Webster* shores up that ribcage. The possibility that one might be the same as what repulses her gives birth to homophobia and nurtures the denial that man and woman can exist in one body, can, in this body, be compassionate, powerful and necessary to community as a whole... Two separate words combined as one. Two spirits in my body. The denial of my existence and the removal of my story is why the holes exist in the bodies of others. I see two spirits, woman/man. The insane fear that one body can house both, drives those afraid of sexuality to hate us. This fear is the reason the search for well-being goes on and why revolution cannot yet occur. I say cannot because I am a Two-Spirited Cree woman. You, who are afraid, need me to be a part of your revolution.

My body, my sexuality, will be at the forefront and in the line of fire. I refuse to sit back. I will not remain silent so someone can escape embarrassment and in doing so escape reality. My monsters loom close by. The childhood voices from within the walls of churches echo countless, meaningless sermons. I look into their eyes and remember I, too, accepted fear as a given. I, too, could not meet my own eyes. I, too, could not exist without my sacred self. To cancel me out you had to sit at the altar. The crime is sitting at the feet of the patriarch while he relaxes on his throne. The offense is gratitude for having been invited to his chambers. The voices of fear, hate and shame will die by their own hands, eventually. The congregation will one day prefer the clean sweet smell of choice rather than the odour of the feet of patriarchy.

Somewhere along the line someone (a white man) decided that his fear of a woman's voice was justified. (The evidence is overwhelming that previous to Contact, homophobia did not exist in my community.) Somewhere along the line his woman agreed and looked at me; told my man to hold his tongue; he, in turn, beat me when I tried to speak. But, I am neither submissive nor passive, and to tell the truth I know no Native woman who is. So, there it is, the connection I have been seeking. The whirlwind grows as masks fall away. There is no separation between the mask of racism and the mask of homophobia.

I will not allow homophobia into my body. I know its claws too well, recognize them when disguised as a woman or a man and have felt its hands around my throat many times. I search for a sensuous being, sift through my own garden, unearth the purple and yellow petals, then expose them to the sunlight. I know that when the earth turns, she does so in the movement of a woman and I hear her voice. Racism/homophobia have found union through marriage and wish me dead. I answer their demands with a simple "no."

Fear of Two-Spirited people originated in the pale hands of racism and the christian belief that man and woman are not equal, that woman should not harbour sensuous being and man's voice is the more knowledgeable. It is based on fear of woman's voice, which carries memory into the present and forward into the future; it is based on the fear that those of us who are brown and Two-Spirited house sacred being. In my lineage I remember. I remember my place, where others have forgotten I stood. I recall every moment so that not one is left behind, so all my voices are brought forward. Only when those who are racist or homophobic (or both) also hear and understand where I have come from will, revolution occur both internally and in the world. On that day, Two-Spirited women and creation will be acknowledged as one. On that day when the earth turns over, you will no longer erase me, institutionalize me, seize my children or condemn me to watch a beloved die of AIDS. In the meantime, here I am and short of putting a bullet through my head, here I stay. Five hundred years could not remove my original place of being and I know that past, present and future are related.

the rock i draped my body across called me to her.
beckoned me to lie with her and recall where i have
come from and the distance i have travelled. into

her roots i sunk, then journeyed into earth's embrace.
she whispered stories to me, allowed me to give
myself to her, sheltered me when the tears arrived.
stone and i are one. i swallowed her beneath a naked
sun. she sits inside smooth and jagged in the same
motion. sun blanketed me, slid down my throat and
warmed my cold. i gave myself to her and in return
she placed herself within my ribcage and accompanied
me to my place of remembering. sun and rock murmured
to me of sensuous being.

I await the day when I am no longer denied a job; no longer rejected by publishers; no longer see fear on the faces of those who hear I am Two-Spirited; watch my son lose friends whose parents have closed minds; no longer told I am not traditional; no longer put on a romantic pedestal when I am no-one's princess; or have to watch my sisters and brothers die of AIDS because fear prevented people from recognizing the familiar hands of genocide. I change "await" to "I refuse to wait" under the umbrella of some-one's complacency, someone's lack of desire to change what lies within them and therefore what surrounds me.

In and Out: Experiences in the Academy

Didi Khayatt

I began my career as a high-school teacher. I taught for a small board in northern Ontario until I quit to do my doctorate in 1980. I mention my beginnings because I lived through the ten years of secondary school teaching with no choice about coming out. Suffice it to say, passing as straight for the sake of my job was a necessity that took its toll, and I finally had to quit. Perhaps it was as a consequence of the ten years of hiding that prompted me to write my doctoral dissertation (which has since become a book) on the subject of my experiences as a school teacher.[1] Perhaps it was a need to make sense of how I had lived in the limbo of existence between passing and being, a place I seem to occupy to different degrees, even when I think I am decisively out. In any case, I am now employed in a university, in a tenure-track position, struggling to make a career within the academy as an out lesbian.

A lifetime of concealing that I am a lesbian from most of my family, my employers and friends in the northern town where I worked, taught me to recognize for myself those cues, those signals that induce me to feel safe in stating the obvious: that I am a lesbian. Coming out is a process in which one engages continually. Most people need constant reminders not to presume heterosexuality. So, while I often think you need just look at me, I mostly have to spell it out to those who will not see me. Given my history, however, I still find it very difficult to make a declarative statement, like "I am a lesbian," mostly because such a statement seems superfluous. My way of coming out is to speak of my life as if my listener is tuned into what I am saying and what I am intending to say. Conversely, in all my written work, published and unpublished, I definitely and unequivocally speak as the lesbian that I am. It is precisely this tension between how I present myself, and in what context and to whom, that I want to address. As a lesbian teacher and scholar, expectations are placed on me.

Last year, I talked to a student who had come out in my class the year before. She had, by then, taken at least three half courses with me, knew my politics and was in the process of doing a directed-studies course with me on lesbian sexuality. During one of those meetings that spoke honestly about our student-teacher relationship, I commented on something she had said, and chose that moment to tell her that I enjoyed working with her. She responded angrily and said that, now that she knew me better, she wanted to mention how she had been greatly annoyed with me for not coming out in class. She had heard about my being a lesbian, and when she finally recognized who I was, she felt disappointed.

I was stunned. Although I had never come out in any of my classes, I was also not in the habit of *speaking* about my private life in my public work, although I write about it ad infinitum. Even though my entire published work is in the area of lesbian and gay studies, my student saw me as "passing," "not out," and somehow lacking in the desired qualities of her ideas of a lesbian academic. While I did not think I was hiding, I was not perceived as being out.

I began to wonder what it meant to be a lesbian academic. It may mean that I am a lesbian who teaches in an academic institution. It may also mean that I am a lesbian who teaches lesbian topics or who includes lesbian/gay materials in her courses of study. Also, It may mean that I am expected to support the lesbian/gay/bisexual student organization on campus, or that I agree to be a speaker in any of the many campus forums. Conversely, it may mean that I am *perceived* to be a "lesbian academic," a term whose definition is beyond my control because it entails not just how I designate myself, but how I conform to a set of expectations and certain types of behaviour that correspond accordingly to the term, in this case, this young woman's notion of a lesbian academic meant that I should be making a spoken statement about my sexuality in class. Finally, it seems to mean that I represent something to those who are observing me. I do not have the privilege of being solely who I want to be, because I am constituted by some of my students as one who has arrived, one who should be using her position as a model.

Several months ago, I talked about my impending paper to my lesbian colleague and friend, who teaches at another institution. She told me that she does not make a practice of coming out in her classes and that one of her lesbian students had been spreading the word around that she is a "sell-out." She asked me: "Do you think we are 'sell-outs,' Didi?"

The question is not whether we are "sell-outs," but who we are perceived to be selling out and to whom. Do I really owe my students a constant visibility? Specifically, do I owe my lesbian or gay students a definite visibility? Do I have to stand out as a lesbian in every aspect of my teaching? Are there real concerns regarding whether I have tenure, whether I can afford to come out, whether I have children to protect (which I do not), whether I have a partner to protect (which I do, since she is a school teacher). The question seems rather to centre on the demands placed on me because of the position I hold.

Furthermore, the question is a political one. Demands are placed on me to make a statement about my sexuality in my classes. Such demands are not made on my heterosexual colleagues. The condition that I should come out as a lesbian implicitly problematizes my sexuality, and not theirs. This is, in some way, understandable because heterosexuality is presumed and homosexuality, if not stated, remains invisible. Therefore, politically speaking, it is necessary to come out in class precisely to challenge heterosexual hegemony and, as some would have us recognize (Garber, 1994; Frye, 1980; Cruikshank, 1982; Klein 1992), to provide "role models" to lesbian and gay students.

Given my own fears, however, the relatively oppressive climate in which I grew up — the pressures to conform, the lack of wholesome models to emulate — I often feel it is imperative for me to be out, to display my sexual orientation as a subversive badge of honour for those not in a position to come out. But, there is no doubt, the issue is more complex than that.

Until last year, I taught on contract in a bilingual college in a very small Women's Studies Program. The college was a hostile environment that was not conducive to coming out as a feminist, let alone, as a lesbian. The program was under a constant barrage of belligerence from colleagues who saw our work as peripheral, not credible, hardly scholarly. I can write at length about teaching in an academic institution where knowledge, truth and scholarship are perceived to be devoid of politics. I can tell you about how women's studies was undervalued and discredited, not just by some colleagues who saw us as using up limited resources, but by our students who put expectations on us they would never dream of demanding from our colleagues in "mainstream" disciplines such as sociology, economics or political science.

The Women's Studies Program where I worked (in a predominantly female environment) was constantly fighting for resources. Although when I was hired, my work indicated that I was a lesbian, my sexuality was never mentioned in the interview. Later, however, whenever I applied for money, produced my *CV* or attended conferences to present papers, it was obvious to my colleagues, to the dean and to most staff members, that my work was entirely within the realm of gay and lesbian studies. Yet I never spoke out about my sexuality, never mentioned my private life, nor talked about myself except to a select few. I wondered whether I "owed it" to my students to come out in class. But I also wondered whether I "owed" it to the Women's Studies Program, already homophobically associated in colleagues' and students' minds with lesbian studies, not to come out. Evelyn Torton Beck expresses well the complex tension between one's need to come out and one's obligation to a vulnerable programme. She says: "I was no longer just a private person or even a professor. I had the responsibility to protect the program's credibility and to build it further, even while maintaining integrity — the program's and mine."[2]

I used to ask my students: "What is frightening about being in women's studies? What makes you afraid of calling yourself a feminist?" The answer was invariably: "Because that would mean I hate men, and if I hate men, I must be a lesbian." To them, being identified with women's studies held its own dangers of "coming out" as a man-hating feminist; to them, it was often a struggle with parents, peers and boyfriends to continue taking courses in the program. Therefore, I often ask myself, how much do I owe to them, to their willingness to risk, to change, and often, to transform their lives. For those women students, it was important that women's studies be constructed as a rigorous, scholarly endeavour, a method, an epistemology, a discipline and not just a radical position with (homo)sexual significations.

I never came out publicly in class at the college where I taught. The complexity of the situation compelled me to question the obligation I felt — a loyalty to a struggling program located in a hostile environment — and to produce it as more benignly conservative than it was. My courses, as were those of my colleagues in women's studies, were strong politically, radical and critical, diverse and different. We raised uncomfortable questions; addressed issues of race, class, sexual orientation, age, ability as these intersected with gender; talked about power relations; and pushed and challenged our students to the limit. And I did it without feeling the need to come out in class.

But I was definitely a disappointment to some of my students. Those who were lesbian or gay had expectations of me I did not meet, ones that I felt I could not meet.

At the end of five years of teaching in that College, I was let go. With me went one third of the program. My courses were dropped because there was no money.

Last year, facing my fifth and last year of contract, I applied to the faculty of education at a university. I was pushed by friends to apply. I had been so convinced then that my contract was going to be transformed into a position that I did not see the necessity of putting myself through the hassle of applying. With this naive belief, I went for my interview at the faculty of education with a brazen attitude, feeling confident that I would not need to accept the position. I had already heard from a friend who teaches at another faculty of education in Southern Ontario that, as she phrased it, "sexual orientation was the last frontier in education — one that is not likely to be crossed too soon." She had even told me that in her particular faculty, they screened teacher candidates so as to make sure no future teacher was gay or lesbian. It was with this forewarning that I went for my interview, certain they would not offer me a job. Feeling I had nothing to lose, I came out in a big way in my interview. I spoke of my partner, my teaching, my politics, my writing, my interests. I sat back and smiled.

They hired me! I was stunned. What I did not, and could not, foresee was the incredible sense of liberation I felt for the first time in my earning life: I was finally able to be who I am in all aspects of my life. I have only taught one year in this faculty, but the feeling is different. I do not have a sense that if I came out, I would in some way undermine the whole field of education. On the contrary, I am a token, I am accepted, I do not have to present my politics, I can just live them and teach them. My colleagues are conscious of my sexuality and, consequently, discussions often include "sexual orientation" as a site of discrimination in the classroom. But, more importantly, I do not have to "reflect" the discipline, I am an integral part of it.

It is within this context of a faculty of education that I am teaching about sexual orientation. Future teachers sit through an integrated course of study that presents them as much about race, class and gender as it does about sexuality.

I do not come out in a stated declaration to my undergraduates unless they ask me, or else they come out to me. I do, however, make my sexuality clear in my graduate course and include my work as a subject of study. But I am still very self-conscious about "who knows" amongst the students. For instance, during the first term this year, one young woman wanted to write her final paper on homosexuality in the classroom. She had clearly indicated to me that she was heterosexual; therefore, I started to wonder why she had chosen such topic. Was it because she *knew?* Was it to please me? In order to end the stress of second-guessing, I asked her. Her reply was unexpected: "My father is gay. I love him, but I could not ever talk about him when I was younger. Now I think I want to understand his choice."

Perhaps more than any other incidents this year, more than the three other students who came out to me, more than my initial sense of liberation, this young woman helped me understand the importance of my place as an out lesbian feminist in the academy.

Endnotes

A version of this paper was presented at the Learned Societies Conference at the University of Calgary, June 3-18, 1994.

1. Didi Khayatt, *Lesbian Teachers: An Invisible Presence* (Albany, NY: State University of New York Press, 1992).

2. Evelyn Torton Beck, "Out as a Lesbian, Out as a Jew" in *Tilting the Tower*, ed. Linda Garber (New York: Routledge, 1994), 228.

Multiple Division: Identity and Integration

Luanne Armstrong

I live in the middle of my own jagged, sharp-edged puzzle. I've been falling apart for years. It's become a habit, hunting for the lost parts, a paper chase in a high wind, my resistance to all the places I go that see only one part of me, to a society and a world as fragmented as exploded glass.

I catch them; I hunt them down, collect them, fit them together. Pieces of my life, my identity, my being as a woman in this time. I catch them and I keep them, and I don't let go. But what makes the puzzle more intriguing is that the shapes change as I get older. New edges appear. New perspectives. Things shift around.

I am travelling with my father in a van for three days; even at forty two, I'm nervous about being alone with him without my mother's mediating influence. We're on our way from BC to the small Saskatchewan town where my grandmother, his mother, is buried. She died when he was seven. His father moved, with my dad and his two sisters, away from the wheat farm, drought and depression, to the B.C. farm where we — our family, parents, my brother and sister-in-law, and occasionally, I — now live.

My father is a "character," a rare type these days, crusty,

gnarled, cussed, a man who can do anything with his hands. This summer, at seventy, he finished building a new house of logs and lumber he cut and sawed himself on his own sawmill. He plants a huge garden, grows tons of fruit, still gets up at 5:30 a.m. to milk. He would do anything for his kids except openly express his love. He feuds gleefully with our ex-suburbanite neighbours, who don't understand the used car junk yard where he finds parts for everything, the giant fires he builds on the mountainside in the winter when he's logging, or his irrigation system drawing water from three creeks on the mountain. There are times he has made me angry enough to wish him dead. I always take the wish back, afraid of my own anger.

Now, sixty years after my grandmother's death, my father and I are going back to a Saskatchewan town to put a headstone on her grave. For some unknown reason, her grave has never been marked. My father and his sisters have finally, this late, bought a stone and made plans to install it. They're embarrassed about waiting so long. Perhaps they've finally realized that they are the only grown-ups in their lives. Somewhat to my own astonishment, I asked to go along. I don't know what I expect, or even why I ask. I am tracking another piece of the puzzle, once again.

Growing up I knew almost nothing of this grandmother apart from the family story of her death; she had died when my father was seven. In this story, and in the only picture we have of her, she was young and beautiful, and talented. She painted watercolours, played the violin and the piano, and loved the dramatic violent landscape of Saskatchewan, a contrast to her sheltered upper middle-class Toronto up-bringing. Her children were nine, seven, and three when she died of cancer, a death so painful she asked my grandfather to kill her. My father had been left with the neighbours and he still can barely stand to talk about the moment they came to tell him his mother had died.

I understood very young how dreadful such a thing would be, to lose a mother. Our mother was the emotional mainstay of our family, where we fled for protection, comfort, advice, food. My father worked long hours to wrestle a living from our small farm. As children, we worked with him, our conversations limited to who had to pick the raspberries that day, who had worked longest and hardest.

My mother wanted to go with us on this trip but she decided she had to can peaches instead. I have not spent any time alone with my father since I was a child. Sitting beside my father is uncomfortable. I am a person who leans on words to make connections; he seldom talks. My mother says, "You're just like your father" meaning she thinks I'm stubborn and opinionated and difficult to manage. He doesn't know who I am. I have no idea if he even wants to know. I know what he does, how he walks, how he will react in most situations, what he will say when I walk in the door after a long time. I know, or I think I know, that he loves me. I think I love him. I don't know what he thinks, or feels. I don't know if I want to know. My father is a presence in my life like weather; contrary, annoying, pervasive.

I hide from him. Even if I explained, would he understand who I am? What label could I choose? Lesbian, writer, environmental organizer, feminist, a person who goes to too many meetings. I can't imagine speaking to my father about my sexuality. I don't even tell him about what work I'm doing. He doesn't know my friends. What does he know? What he sees is what I let him see. The rest, I think he would neither understand nor approve.

No, more than that. I'm afraid he'd hate it. I'm afraid

he'd hate me. And there are no words between us I can trust to explain who I am to him.

Yet so much of what I know comes from him, to be strong, tough, to care for land and animals, to survive.

When I ride beside him in the van, my body is tight, clenched, curled in on itself like a fist. I feel twelve, instead of forty. I don't know what I'm afraid of. My father, as far as I can remember, was not physically abusive, except that our mealtimes were marked by his teasing, and his tickling, especially me, his favourite target. My mother screamed at him to leave us alone. I didn't like or hate being tickled. I never knew I could tell him no. I always assumed he had a right to do what he wanted. My body belonged to him.

Being a lesbian means, in some sense I don't fully understand, saying no to my father. I wept after my first time making love with a woman. What I felt, for the first time in my life, was safe. And despite my forty years and my strength and my knowledge and my awareness, I sit, now, on the edge of my seat, trying to look relaxed.

We're here together because we're family. We're connected through blood and genetics and history and culture. We're a rural family, an extended family, self-sufficient, quaint, archaic in our ways. We still live close together, grow almost all our own food, live as we've always done, out of habit and because, in our isolated area, with 40 to 50 per cent chronic unemployment, it's a way to survive. Survival is in our blood. "Work," my father thundered at his kids. "Work or starve." Poverty is in our blood, so is desperation; we're rooted in our land, and arrogant about it. The arrogance of land-rich, money-poor rural people, detesting the suburban world that moves closer to us year by year.

The rest of my family — my brother and sisters — know me as little as my father. We are all very different. My sister shoes and trains horses. One brother is a logger, one a social worker. I am the only one who has made it through university. My mother and I talk a lot about family. We're clannish, we tell each other. We don't like "outsiders," strangers, city people, people with a lot of money. We hate tourists. I have lectured my kids that our sense of ourselves as a family is important, something to work on and maintain. We are a "close" family; thus we believe. We live in each other's pockets; family dinners, celebrations, work projects. Over the years, we have fought often, loudly, cruelly, and made up when we got tired of fighting.

As the years go by, we hang on to each other, but we still don't talk much. We talk about farming and weather and community gossip. What we have in common is bonds of blood and shared history. But what sustains this shared identity, other than our complicit agreement to sustain it, is increasingly a mystery to me. On this trip I am looking for this piece of the puzzle, some part of this elusive mystery which bonds us, our family. Some days I don't even know what the word means. Yet I cling to the word, and the idea.

While I'm in this van, sweating in the August heat, sugar beet fields, wheat fields, hay fields, herds of red or white or black cattle, rush by and disappear into hazy memory. I notice the crops. I notice the land, the water. My father and I can, at least, talk about them.

When we get to the tiny grey town in Saskatchewan, we stay with an elderly couple who are somewhere around sixth cousins to my father. We have brought them fruit from the farm. I spend the evening washing and sorting and freezing fruit, listening to my father and his sisters and the couple; I am left out of the conversation, relegated to being younger. The next day I make biscuits and a stew for lunch, familiar farm food. Comfortable in this elderly woman's kitchen, I fetch beets and carrots from the garden. This is the kind of food I grew up on, what I fed my children. We sit around after lunch and talk about crops and weather and who used to live here and who moved away and who still knows and keeps in touch with who. I feel at home here. The lesbian feminist part of me crouches in a corner, muttering nervously to herself. The biscuits are a big hit. Our hostess has won blue ribbons at the fall fair for her biscuits.

The cemetery is small, flat, enclosed by a white fence. The long grass outside the fence and the carefully tended flower beds inside it bend in the hot prairie wind. When we stand at the graveside and lay flowers on the new stone, I surprise myself by weeping. I stand at the grave, mourning and trying to hold it back. I want to sit down and howl, but I don't. I don't know what I'm crying about. I want some prayers, a ritual, something to make this meaningful, understandable, something to put it in place. I am grieving and not sure what it is I'm grieving. Is it for my father or for myself?

My father and his sisters are solemn but not sad. I stand, blurry-eyed, in the sun, with the hot dry wind tugging my hair, in this town my grandmother came to from the ranch when she was finally dying. She lived for another three weeks in the tiny local hospital. My father remembers her as happy, as a woman who loved her new home, loved the prairies, loved this same wind, this wide blue sky.

But her death left my father a legacy of grief, never spoken, but which I also feel. This man whose life has shaped mine, a man I'm afraid of, a man whose footsteps I walked in when I was little, trying to match his enormous strides as we went around the farm together. A man whose footsteps on the back porch my mother and I both dreaded, who usually came in the house angry, ranting, furious.

A man I am like. The man, I say, only half-joking, who taught me to be a dyke, taught me strength, independence, toughness, cussedness. I learned because I had to fight him to survive. And in that lifelong fight, I've recognized the parts of myself that come from him.

We lay bouquets of flowers on the grave. I leave a stone from our farm in BC. Then it's done. We leave. That night, during dinner at the local hotel, the waitress recognizes my father's name in the guest book and comes over. "We were in grade one together," she says to my father. Almost everyone in the dining room is elderly, except for one young couple with children, and they, it turns out, are the grandchildren of two local farm families. They have stayed, married each other, taken up farming.

The next morning, we get back in the van for the long drive home. I drive most of the way home. My father sleeps in the opposite seat. He always sleeps easily, naps in his chair at home. I drive through the dark and the rain, back into my life, the one I've created, making plans to spend time with the woman I love, to go back to my far-away job. The dislocated pieces of my life drift and tangle around me. Children, work, lover, family, land.

I think, perhaps, we should have a family reunion. I don't know the children of my father's family, of his cousins. I make plans to write to my own cousins, who I have not seen since they were children, and haven't thought about for years, and tell them about this trip, about our grandmother. I am trying to remember how I feel about them; did we like each other as children; do we have anything still in common? I dream about my lover, who also lives far away. I am going to see her next week. And then I'm leaving her, too, to go to work, in another place, far away from both my family and my lover. My father's breathing fills the interior of the van. The rain streaks in question marks on the glass.

My grandfathers were farmers, as I am, when I can afford time at home, at the farm. The fathers, the men. The family stories are about them. I know little about the women, their wives. I miss my grandmother's history. The ironic contradiction at the heart of my grieving, recognizing the value of this heritage, and still missing the parts that have been left out.

As a feminist, I want to remake the world these men made and left to me. As their child, I inherit it and the values and strengths that are there for me to find. As their child, when I stand in the garden, when I bend, when I walk, with animals, pruning trees, I feel their voices in my bones, and I know what I'm doing.

I flail at these men and their righteousness and authority in their world. My father never questioned their world. I do it for him, and for myself making a bridge in this dark night between the fractured pieces of my reality, going home to the farm where I walk on land that was my grandfather's and will be my children's. When I leave, I work in another place, where I claim my feminist label, a world where occasionally, I can even be free to walk into a room as a lesbian, a world in which to ask questions, to write, to organize, to study, to learn. But a world where the rich and rooted culture I come from and love is lost, invisible. Where I wander, in many places, most of me is submerged and quiet. I never stay in any place for long and I always come back home to the farm, the place which claims me, chains me, holds me still, holds my heart.

I don't understand why I miss her so much, this other unknown woman, my long dead grandmother. Wishful thinking that if she had lived, she would have been someone who could see me. And if she had lived, would my father have been different? Would I have been different? I imagine it is her I am like. I imagine she would have loved me, told me stories. I miss who we could have been together. There is a gap, a hole, left by her death.

I drive through the night, invisible even to myself, wanting, wanting, wanting, everything: the whole ball of wax, the whole kit and kaboodle, my family, my friends, my lover, my work, my community, heritage, roots, branches, leaves and all. All the bright mysterious pieces of my life lie around me and greedy, I want them all. I want them whole, unfractured, unsplit, without these multiple divisions, without the losses, the gaping holes in our lives, in my life.

Despite everything, we're here, I'm here, our family stays together. We all go on trying, maintaining the ties between us. Perhaps it's the most I can expect for now, until the world shifts again. I don't want to let go or divest myself of any of the pieces of myself, no matter how much easier it might be to do so. Nor do I want to be owned by any of them. I am all over the map, my own map, where each piece fits, where borders shift and change but the ground itself is ancient; where I am rooted, where I have grown from, and where I return.

Up The Token Pole

**(excerpted from the keynote address
to OutWrite 1993)**

Chrystos

Writing happens in the cracks of my life. My books are shed
snake skins of my fierce journey toward justice and safety
for the First Nations, called Indians. Though I have been a
proud femme dyke for twenty-nine years, my first concern
as an activist is for my People. This separates me profoundly
from the queer community, who for the most part, are
indifferent to our prisoners of war, the conditions of our
lives and the facts of our existence. We have the highest
infant mortality rate in the western hemisphere, the highest
teenage suicide rate in the world and the average life span
for a Native Nations woman is forty-five years. This year I
will celebrate my forty-seventh birthday with a passion it
may be hard for you to imagine, because I am the survivor
of the deaths of five lesbians in my friendship/family circle
from breast cancer, all of whom were women of colour. And
of the eighty original members of Gay American Indians in
San Francisco, only twenty survive, because of AIDS and
breast cancer.

I write from a desperation of survival that sees privilege
as a barrier to our unity. I don't write to buy a bmw or to be
famous. I write, literally, against the enormous machine of

erasure and genocide that is the colonizers' final solution for Native Americans. I would suggest to you that, as we queers become more politically active for groups other than ourselves, we will lose more and more of our complacency, and the u.s. will have a final solution for queers as well.

I am at war with heterosexual colonization as surely as I am at war against greed and ignorance. Traditionally in our Nations, Two-Spirited persons were very sacred. Our roles were various. We mediated disputes between men and women, gave names, acted as healers and philosophers and dreamers. In some of our nations, these roles are active today. As an example, my good friend Wesley Thomas is a traditional Navajo or Diné Two-Spirit who is honoured and respected among his People. His mother weaves dresses for him. Most of us have been deeply wounded by dominant culture because we've never experienced this kind of love. We can use this understanding to create writing and art, which would bring more love into our lives. We can speak the truth of our battles and use this power of words to claim our natural place in human life.

Writers have serious responsibilities to honour our connections to each other and to our home and mother, the earth. Writing is not a right or an ego trip, but a profoundly sacred act. We must be very careful in what we create, continuously examining the meanings of our acts and our metaphors. Words can be used to demean, to justify injustice, to confuse and to attack. As colonized people — and each of us is colonized — we have a womandate to examine our own hearts as we write. Everyone has written scathing replies to ex-lovers, as I have. But we don't publish those because we understand that it doesn't heal. That is our work: to heal all the splits and divisions among people. Because we live outside of gender cliches, we are uniquely qualified to do this work. We need to keep our minds alert and whole. I joke that I am a honosexual because I have such good sharp sex.

We have the opportunity now, unique in written western history, to engage our passion in the struggle for equality, a concept which has never been actualized against the zombies of columbozo colonization. We face dangerous phrases and words which must be eliminated. The concept of "political correctness" has been abused until our natural understanding of justice has become lost in embarrassment. We know that discrimination and violence are morally wrong. But the ruling corporations find it inconvenient for us to have a conscience and set about to destroy our common sense with glitzy advertising, lies, mockery and co-optation.

Because we don't agree with the myths of what little girls or boys are made of, we are dangerous to the status quo. I believe it is very silly to want to be accepted by the so-called mainstream. I think they need to be accepted by us. They have a long hard job ahead of them.

Another phrase which is a tool of oppressors is "ethnic cleansing." I could not believe it when I first saw that phrase roll out of a newscaster's mouth. I posit to you that there is no such thing as clean murder. These phrases are from con artists whose job is to convince us to accept injustice. As long as we butcher language ourselves, such as using the word, "blind," to mean ignorance or insensitivity, we are cooperating with our oppressors. When we hold events in inaccessible places or charge rates that could buy a bag of groceries, we imitate the very people whose aim it is to eliminate us.

What people of colour, the aged and imprisoned, those with disabilities, share with us, as queers, is our outsider status. When we fight only to have our own private privilege, we are betraying our comrades and denying our sacred role as healers. These issues that I am naming are often dismissed as tiresome. I challenge you to think about what it means when equality and mutual respect are considered boring.

One of my particular jobs is to spread the word about Norma Jean Croy, a Native lesbian who remains incarcerated, though her brother has been freed on the grounds of self-defence in the same incident. This is a reflection of the fact that the prison business is blatantly sexist and racist, routinely forcing women and people of colour to serve double and triple time compared to white males. To receive more information on her case, or to make donations (which are much needed) please contact:

Norma Jean Croy Defense Committee
Pier 5
San Francisco, California
USA 94111

A video, called *Shasta Woman*, is also available from the Defense Committee for a donation of $15.00 to $25.00 (u.s. funds), which includes postage. You may write directly to Norma Jean at:

Norma Jean Croy
CCWF #14293
Box 1508
Chowchilla, California
USA 93610

I close with a poem I wrote for the place where I live, to give you the gift of open sky, to carry you safely on your journey.

Before Me the Land & Water Open

their arms tender sisters who have kept my place
watched each spray of racing birds
woven them into the still air for me to catch
a shimmering glint
The blowzy pine grows tall
as the distant mountains we call home
Mischief of the eye is sweet
Silver slate the Sound ruffles my hair
Roots I have packed for years settle in this meadow
delicate with brambles, broom
bright yellow suns I call beach daisies
These are the shapes I dream in hotel rooms
These are the variations of green & gold
I keep deep within my hands
These never same astounding clouds drift through my eyes
in bleached conversations with strangers
These are the leaves & berries who marry me in delight
This is the earth I carry in a corn husk pouch
against the brutal light of clapping hands
Here is the path choked with driftwood I trace
to watch the sun go down over mountains whose wildflowers
have caught & pressed my heart
Fly through these words sharp as
a deep blue & rust swallow
that wavering branch is
waiting for you

Megwetch,
which means thank you in my language.

Bibliography

Beck, Evelyn Torton, ed. *Nice Jewish Girls — A Lesbian Anthology.* Boston, MA: Beacon Press, 1989.

—. "Out as a Lesbian, Out as a Jew." In *Tilting the Tower,* edited by Linda Garber, 228. New York: Routledge, 1994.

Bendt, Ingela. *We Shall Return — Women in Palestine.* London, England: Zed Press Ltd., 1980.

Border/Lines: Canada's Magazine of Cultural Studies. no. 32. (winter 1994).

Bulkin, Elly, Minnie Bruce Pratt, and Barbara Smith. *Yours in Struggle: Three Feminist Perspectives on Anti-Semitism and Racism.* Ithaca, New York: Firebrand Books, 1988.

Butler, Sandra, and Barbara Rosenblum. *Cancer in Two Voices.* San Francisco: Spinsters, 1991.

Calhoun, Jackie. *Lifestyles.* Tallahassee, Florida: Naiad Press, 1990.

Carby, Hazel V. *Reconstructing Womanhood: The Emergence of the Afro-American Woman Novelist.* New York: Oxford University Press, 1987.

Collins, Patricia Hill. *Black Feminist Thought: Knowledge, Consciousness, and the Politics of Empowerment.* London: Harper Collins, 1990.

de Lauretis, Theresa. "Queer theory: Lesbian and gay sexualities — An introduction," *differences* (summer 1991): iv.

Felman, Shoshana, and Dori Laub. *Testimony: Crises of Witnessing in Literature, Psychoanalysis, and History.* New York: Routledge, 1992.

Feinberg, Leslie. *Stone Butch Blues.* Ithaca: Firebrand Books, 1993.

Fireweed: A Feminist Quarterly of Art, Politics and Culture. no. 35 (spring 1992).

Fireweed: A Feminist Quarterly of Art, Politics and Culture. no. 42 (winter 1994).

Forrest, Katherine V. *An Emergence of Green.* Tallahassee, Florida: Naiad Press, 1986.

Frankenburg, Ruth. *White Women, Race Matters: The Social Construction of Whiteness.* Minneapolis: University of Minnesota Press, 1993.

''From the Mouth to the Page'' *Fireweed: A Feminist Quarterly* of Art, Politics and Culture. no. 39 (summer 1993).

Fuss, Diana, ed. *Inside/Out: Lesbian Theories, Gay Theories.* New York: Routledge, 1991.

Gilman, Sander L. *Difference and Pathology: Stereotypes of Sexuality, Race, and Madness.* Ithaca: Cornell University Press, 1985.

hooks, bell. *Black Looks: Race and Representation.* Boston: South End Press, 1992.

Jewish Women's Committee to End the Occupation of the West Bank and Gaza. *Jewish Women's Call For Peace: A Handbook for Jewish Women on the Israeli/Palestinian Conflict.* Ithaca, New York: Firebrand Books, 1990.

Johanna, H. H. *Romancing the Dream.* New York: Rising Tide Press, 1991.

Johnston, Jill. *Lesbian Nation.* New York: Random House, 1973.

Kaye/Kantrowitz, Melanie. *The Issue is Power — Essays on Women, Jews, Violence and Resistance.* San Francisco, CA: aunt lute books, 1992.

Kennedy, Evelyn. *Cherished Love.* Tallahassee, Florida: Naiad Press, 1988.

Khayatt, Didi. *Lesbian Teachers: An Invisible Presence.* Albany, NY: State University of New York Press, 1992.

Kinsman, Gary. *The Regulation of Desire.* Montreal, Black Rose, 1987.

Klepfisz, Irena. *Dreams of an Insomniac: Jewish Feminist Essays, Speeches and Diatribes.* Portland, Oregon: Eighth Mountain Press, 1990.

Lindenbaum, Joyce P. ''The Shattering of an Illusion: The Problem of Competition in Lesbian Relationships,'' *Feminist Studies* 11, no. 1 (spring 1985): 96-97.

Lorde, Audre. *The Cancer Journals.* San Francisco: Spinsters, 1980.

Love, Susan M., with Karen Lindsey. *Dr. Susan Love's Breast Book.* New York: Addison-Wesley, 1990.

MacCowan, Lyndall. ''Recollecting history, renaming lives: Femme stigma and the feminist seventies and eighties.'' In *The Persistent Desire: A Femme-Butch Reader,* edited by Joan Nestle, 322. Boston: Alyson Publications, 1992.

McIntosh, Peggy. ''White Privilege: Unpacking the Invisible Knapsack.'' *Peace and Freedom,* July / August, 1989.

Minatoya, Lydia Yuriko *Talking to High Monks in the Snow, An Asian American Odyssey.* New York: Harper Collins Publishers, Inc., 1992.

Mossop, Brian ''Brian Mossop Responds,'' *Xtra,* no. 219, March 19, 1993, 29.

Panzarino, Connie. *The Me in the Mirror.* Seattle: Seal Press, 1994.

Penelope, Julia. *Call Me Lesbian.* California: Crossing Press, 1992.

Pollock, Griselda, public lecture, ''Strategies of Dissonance,'' The Mendel Art Gallery, Saskatoon, Sask., May 6, 1994.

Rich, Adrienne. ''Compulsory heterosexuality and lesbian existence.'' In *Powers of Desire,* edited by Ann Snitow, Christine Stansell, and Sharon Thompson, 177-208. New York: Monthly Review Press, 1983.

Roscoe, Will. *The Zuni Man-Woman. Taos*: University of New Mexico Press.

Rubin, Gayle. ''The traffic in women: Notes on the political economy of sex.'' In *Towards an Anthropology of Women,* edited by Rayna R. Reiter, 157-210. New York, Monthly Review Press, 1975.

Siegal, Rachel Josefowitz, *Jewish Women in Therapy: Seen But Not Heard.* London, England: 1990.

Sinister Wisdom (winter 1992/93).

Tanaka, Yukiko, ed. *To Live and To Write, Selections by Japanese Women Writers, 1913-1938.* Seattle: Seal Press, 1987.

Vance, Carole. ''Gender Systems, Ideology and Sex Research,'' In *Powers of Desire, The Politics of Sexuality,* edited by Ann Snitow, Christine Stansell, and Sharon Thompson, 375-376. New York: Monthly Review Press, 1983.

Van Every, Jo. ''Who is the 'family'? The assumptions of British social policy,'' p. 4. Revised version of paper presented at the Canadian Sociology and Anthropology Association Annual Conference, Queen's University, Kingston, Ontario, June 1-4, 1991.

Warland, Betsy, ed. *InVersions — Writing by Dykes, Queers, Lesbians.* Vancouver: Press Gang Publishers, 1991.

Wittig, Monique. *The Straight Mind.* Boston: Beacon Press, 1992.

Contributors

Mary Louise Adams is a writer and teacher living in Toronto. She is currently working on a book about sexuality and sports..

Luanne Armstrong is a white, feminist, farmer, lesbian, of Scottish/Celtic descent. She presently lives with her extended family on a subsistence organic farm in BC. She has previously published one book of poetry, as well as short stories, essays and poems. She is writing a series of essays on race, gender, and environmental issues. Her first novel will be published in the spring, 1995.

karen/miranda augustine is a bisexual, Black woman of Dominican and Carib Indian heritage. A Toronto-based writer and visual artist, her work has been featured in several anthologies, feminist and art publications, including *Fireweed, Fuse* and *Gallerie*. She is the founder and managing editor of *At the Crossroads: A Journal for Women Artists of African Descent*. Currently, she is editing a book, *EYES ON THIS: Africanadian Perspectives on Art, Media, Politics and Culture*.

Sheila Batacharya lives in Toronto where she goes to school and works with other South Asian dykes in the production of *Sami Yoni: A Journal for Lesbians of South Asian Descent.*

Maureen Bradley is a video maker/artist. She is a graduate student in Media Studies and is completing a video examining the media coverage of the killings at the École Polytechnique in Montréal. Her videos have screened throughout the international queer film and video festival circuit. She is programming co-coordinator for *Out On The Screen*, Vancouver's lesbian and gay film and video festival.

Beth Brant is a Bay of Quinte Mohawk from Tyendinaga Mohawk Territory in Ontario. She is the editor of *A Gathering of Spirit*, the ground-breaking collection of writing and art by Native women. She is the author of *Mohawk Trail* (Women's Press/Firebrand Books), prose and poetry, and *Food & Spirits* (Press Gang/Firebrand Books), short fiction. She is also the author of *Writing as Witness* (Women's Press) a collection of essays. Her work has appeared in numerous Native, feminist and lesbian anthologies and she has done readings, lectures and taught throughout North America. She divides her time between living in Michigan and in Canada. She is a mother and grandmother and lives with her partner of eighteen years, Denise Dorsz. She has been writing since the age of forty and considers it a gift for her community.

Elise Chenier is a writer and is currently studying the history of sexuality in Canada at Queen's University.

Chrystos, self-educated, born in San Francisco in 1946 of Menominee & Euro-immigrant parents, now living on an island in Puget Sound. Author of *Not Vanishing, Dream On, In Her I Am* (dyke erotica) & the forthcoming *Fugitive Colors*. Winner of the Audre Lorde International Competition sponsored by Cleveland State University Poetry Center.

I work as a maid, read and give writing workshops in prisons, universities, bookstores and bars. I've been a dyke for 29 years, one of over 200 Native/First Nations Two-Spirit women on the North American continent. Sober since 1988. My favorite (& most common) review is the remark, "I hate poetry, but I like yours."

Ann Decter is a white bisexual of Jewish and Irish descent. Her first novel, *Paper, Scissors, Rock* (Press Gang) was published in 1992 and she is working on a sequel. She is a co-editor of *Out Rage: Dykes & BIs Resist Homophobia* and works as a co-managing editor at Women's Press in Toronto.

Rachel Epstein lives in Toronto with her lover/partner/friend Lois Fine, their daughter Sadie Rose Epstein-Fine, and their part-time son Aaron. The blending of her personal and political visions have led her to wear many hats, although motherhood definitely restricts the numbers. She currently works primarily as a teacher and as a mother.

Dionne Falconer is a Black bisexual feminist working in the Black community around AIDS prevention and support.

Connie Fife writes as an indian lesbian living in a racist, homophobic society. "when i am quiet it is not because i am allowing myself to be further victimised, but rather i, too, await my own eruptions." Her poetry collection, *Beneath the Naked Sun*, was published by Sister Vision Press in 1993, as was *The Colour of Resistance*, an collection of writing by First Nations women which she anthologized.

barbara findlay is a lesbian feminist lawyer, raised in a working-class family of Scots Presbyterian and English heritage on the prairies. She is passionate about learning how to work across the differences among us.

Alisa Gayle-Deutsch is a bi-racial, Jewish Lesbian currently involved in several political, community and social activism groups in Toronto (and is attempting a degree in Women's Studies and Jewish Studies at University of Toronto). She is thankful for all of the special, loving women in her life who believe in and work for wholeness everyday.

Sheila Gilhooly is a white 43-year-old mad dyke living in Vancouver. She is working for our welcome in the world, and she figures that before we can be welcomed, we have to be seen. So she is as visible as a lesbian as she knows how to be.

Candis Graham: Two collections of my stories have been published, *Imperfect Moments* (Polestar Books, 1993) and *Tea For Thirteen* (Impertinent Press, 1990). My first novel will be published in 1995, and I am working on another collection of stories and one of essays. This essay is dedicated to three freedom fighters — Wendy Clouthier and Margaret Telegdi and Marie Robertson.

Didi Khayatt teaches at the Faculty of Education at York University. She is interested in issues of gender, race relations and sexuality. She is the author of a number of articles and her first book, *Lesbian Teachers: An Invisible Presence*, was published by SUNY Press in 1992. She is currently involved in research in the area of sexual categories.

Lori Lyons is a Toronto lesbian and activist, who writes sporadically and has been published in the Toronto papers, *Quota* and *Xtra*. She learned to write under an assumed name in the underground queer 'zine *In Your Face*. A founding member of the now defunct Queer Nation Toronto, she devotes much of her political energy to AIDS Action Now!. She is constantly inspired by a supportive network of friends, her lover Kaz and her lover's daughter Krista.

Kathleen Martindale is associate professor of English at York University where she teaches and writes about lesbian and feminist literary and cultural theory. She is writing a book entitled *Unpopular Culture: Lesbian Writing After the Sex Wars*.

Mona Oikawa's first book, *All Names Spoken* was published by Sister Vision Press in 1992. Her poetry, short stories, and essays have been published in *Privileging Sites: Positions in Asian American Studies*, *The Very Inside*, *Out Rage*, and other anthologies. Frequent visits to the ocean and the mountains help to sustain her life and work in Toronto.

Concetta (Connie) Panzarino was born in 1947 and is a lesbian with a progressive neuro-muscular disease which allows her only movement of her right thumb and facial muscles. She earned a BA from Hofstra University in 1969, and holds a Master's degree in Art Therapy from New York University. She is a practicing Registered Art Therapist working with both men and women survivors of physical and sexual abuse, lectures nationwide on the subjects of disability, homophobia, sexism, the ethics of genetic engineering, and is a professional artist. Because her disability is beginning to limit some of her travel to conferences and speaking engagements, she decided to write her autobiography. *The Me in The Mirror* (Seal Press, 1994) serves to educate persons with and about disabling conditions. She has also co-authored *Rebecca Finds a New Way*, a book for children with spinal cord injuries and spinal cord diseases.

Deborah L. Repplier is a white lesbian feminist who believes in labeling — sometimes. She calls herself poet and fiction writer, and has recently co-edited and published *Our Writes*, an anthology of women's voices. She has an M.A. in English Literature and teaches writing at the University of Massachusetts, Boston.

Judith P. Stelboum is associate professor of literature and women's studies at the City University of New York, College of Staten Island. She has had fiction, poetry and essays published in *Common Lives/Lesbian Lives* and *Sinister Wisdom*. A review and discussion of five books of lesbian erotica appears in the premier issue of *The Lesbian Review of Books*. An autobiographical piece about the process of coming out is included in the anthology *Sister and Brother*. A short story, "Her Sister's Wedding," will be published by Alyson Press in an anthology of lesbian and gay writing for young adults.

Ann Yuri Ueda is a sansei (third-generation Japanese American) lesbian who lives in San Francisco, California. Her writing has appeared in the *Asian Pacific American Journal; Outrage: Dykes and Bis Resist Homophobia* (Women's Press); and *The Very Inside,* an anthology of writing by Asian and Pacific Islander lesbian and bisexual women (Sister Vision Press). Currently, she divides her time between studying the 2,000 kanji necessary to be literate in

Japanese and writing new material for a one-woman performance. In 1996 she plans to travel to and live in Japan for the first time, while working on her first book detailing her experiences in Asia.

Poet, essayist, editor and playwright **Betsy Warland**'s most recent books are *The Bat Had Blue Eyes* (Women's Press, 1993) and *Two Women in a Birth* (in collaboration with Daphne Marlatt, Guernica Editions, 1994). She edited *InVersions: Writing by Dykes, Queers and Lesbians* (Press Gang, 1991), which is the first anthology of North American lesbian writers writing about their own work.

Having earned an M.A. in Creative Writing, **Diane Williams** is a full-time English instructor at the College of Lake County in Grayslake, Illinois. Her fiction and poetry have appeared in a number of publications, including *West Side Stories, The Country of Herself,* and *Columbia Poetry Review.* In 1992 her play, ''Women on the Wing,'' won the Best Production Prize at the Love Creek Productions Playwrights Festival in New York; and her poem, ''Portrait of Paradox,'' was co-recipient of the Pat Parker Poetry Award that same year.

Photo: Ka Yin Fong

Dionne Falconer, Mona Oikawa and Ann Decter